20 Questions about Ministry

20 Questions about Ministry

JAMES CUNNEEN

RESOURCE *Publications* • Eugene, Oregon

20 QUESTIONS ABOUT MINISTRY

Copyright © 2018 James Cunneen. All rights reserved. Except for brief quotations in critical publications or reviews, no part of this book may be reproduced in any manner without prior written permission from the publisher. Write: Permissions, Wipf and Stock Publishers, 199 W. 8th Ave., Suite 3, Eugene, OR 97401.

Resource Publications
An Imprint of Wipf and Stock Publishers
199 W. 8th Ave., Suite 3
Eugene, OR 97401

www.wipfandstock.com

PAPERBACK ISBN: 978-1-5326-5468-8
HARDCOVER ISBN: 978-1-5326-5469-5
EBOOK ISBN: 978-1-5326-5470-1

Manufactured in the U.S.A. 09/05/18

Unless otherwise noted, "Scripture quotations are taken from the New American Standard Bible ©, Copyright © 1960, 1962, 1963, 1968, 1971, 1972, 1973, 1975, 1977, 1995 by The Lockman Foundation. Used by permission" (www.lockman.org)

Some Scripture quotations noted by "NIV" are taken from The Holy Bible, New International Version©. Copyright © 1973, 1978, 1984 by International Bible Society. Used by permission of Zondervan Publishing House. All rights reserved.

The "NIV" and "New International Version" trademarks are registered in the United States Patent and Trademark Office by International Bible Society. Use of either trademark requires the permission of International Bible Society.

To my daughter, Jennifer
a servant of God

&

the Life To Life Ministry team

Contents

Preface ix

1. **God has put it on my heart to do ministry; how do I get started?** 1
2. **How do I know what kind of ministry God is calling me to?** 10
3. **How do I lead a small-group Bible study?** 18
4. **How do I share the gospel relationally?** 29
5. **What are tough issues non-Christians bring up?** 42
   - "If God is so loving, why is there pain and evil in the world?"
   - "Hasn't history shown that 'truth' is relative?"
   - "What about people who don't hear about Christ?"
6. **What are evidences for the existence of God?** 52
7. **How can I feel confident that I'm interpreting the Bible correctly?** 58
8. **What is worship?** 70
9. **How do I advise people in ministry about the decisions they face?** 76
10. **What are issues that Christians ask about?** 84
    - "What's my spiritual gift?"
    - "What did Jesus change?"
    - "What are laborers for the harvest?"
    - "Explain the predestination and free will issue."
11. **How do I find good people to disciple?** 99

12. What's the Bible say about submission to authority?	106
13. Can we hurt people in ministry?	111
14. Do people really change?	118
15. What would you say to professors in seminaries?	123
16. Why doesn't God help us more in ministry?	126
17. Why don't more Christians do this?	131
18. How do I help people in the ministry with problems?	138
19. What does "success" in ministry look like?	148
20. How can I keep going?	151
Bibliography	157

Preface

THE APOSTLE PAUL SAID it best. *For who is our hope or joy or crown of exultation? Is it not even you . . . ?* (1 Thessalonians 2:19)

There are few joys in life comparable to that of Christian ministry: sharing Christ with others, and helping younger Christians to grow. This book is offered to encourage those who are ministering—or want to minister—for the glory of God and the increase of His Kingdom.

These are 20 key questions—of the many questions that have arisen—to which I'd like to suggest answers. I hope the discussions about these issues will be helpful.

I'm not going to present these as if they are specific questions from individuals— i.e. "J. L. from Raleigh, NC asks, ' What about such and such?'"— but rather as generic, though real, questions about ministry that have occurred numerous times—e.g. "How do I lead a good small-group Bible study?"

While this book can be read sequentially, from Questions 1 to 20, it's really intended more as a resource to address whatever ministry issue may have arisen. So please feel free to skim the Table of Contents and go to the question that seems most relevant.

I hope these topics will be both encouraging and challenging.

–James Cunneen

Question 1

God has put it on my heart to do ministry; how do I get started?

GOD IS WELL PLEASED when Christians want to serve Him. One of the clearest statements of this is found, I think, in the Lord's words in John 17:18, *As you sent Me into the world, I send them into the world.* It's a transfer of a job description. We Christians have a job—His job. And His instruction is *to . . . make disciples of all nations . . . teaching them to obey all I have commanded . . .* (Matthew 28:19,20)

Since these words are inspired Scripture, we can assume they apply to us today as well as to the original disciples. Otherwise, we're just reading someone else's mail.

If you desire to serve God, but aren't sure what specific kind of ministry God wants you to do, you might want to skip ahead to Question 2: *What kind of ministry is God calling me to?*

There are different types of ministry, as noted in 1 Corinthians 12:5,6 *. . . there are varieties of ministries, and the same Lord. And there are varieties of effects, but the same God who works all things . . .*

For the purpose of this question, however, we'll describe a disciple-making ministry that (primarily) involves adults. This focus will probably be relevant to most ministries, as many types of ministry involve helping people become more knowledgeable and godly, and that's a big part of disciple-making.

Remember, a common essential that applies to all types of ministry is this—your own walk with God must be solid. Effective ministry comes out of the *overflow* of one's relationship with God.

> *Abide in Me and I in you. As the branch cannot bear fruit of itself, unless it abides in the vine, so neither can you, unless you abide in Me . . . he who abides in Me, and I in him, he bears much fruit . . . By this is My Father glorified, that you bear much fruit, and so prove to be My disciples. . (John 15:4–8)*

The powerful implication of Christ's words is a sense of *inevitability* of fruitfulness for believers who have a close, obedient relationship with the Lord. In agriculture, an orange tree with no fruit is either immature, diseased, or dead. A healthy, mature tree bears fruit. That's its nature. A healthy mature Christian bears fruit. That's our nature, through the enabling of God.

Let's quickly look at Jesus' ministry during His time on earth. We see that the Lord did four essential activities. And we can pattern our own personal ministry after His.

1. He ministered to the many . . .
2. He selected the few . . .
3. He spent personal time with the few, and imparted His life to them . . .
4. He trained the few for service, so they could do the same for others.

While you will most likely not find yourself feeding 5000 with a few loaves and fishes, you can involve yourself with a group of people (the "many") whom you can teach and from whom you can select a few to disciple. Here are four simple stages—similar to Jesus' ministry—you can do to have a fruitful personal ministry:

- find a good local church
- lead a small group
- pick a faithful one or two
- help that person to grow in a way that is reproducible (or pass-on-able)

That's it!

Find a good local church to use as the base of your ministry. Hopefully, you're already involved in a good local church; maybe that's a key reason you're interested in ministry. But it's helpful to quickly evaluate if a particular church is the place in which you can conduct a fruitful personal ministry.

How do I do that? There are many factors that contribute to a church being one you benefit from, and to which you can contribute. The needs of your family (e.g. good children's programs) and proximity are just a couple. But here's a little acronym that may serve as a starting point:

Go to the *"B.E.S.T"* church you can find. A good local church has at least these attributes:

- B = *Bible* . . . does the church proclaim and teach clear biblical truth, without denominational bias or liberal influence? (2 Timothy 3: 16,17) *All scripture is inspired by God and profitable for teaching, reproof, correction, and training in righteouness . . .*

- E = *Encouragement* . . . does going to this church encourage you— through the music, messages from the pastor, and the fellowship of the other believers? (Hebrews 10: 24,25) *Let us consider how to stir up one another to love and good works . . . encouraging one another . . .*

- $ . . . (sorry for the sneaky symbolism) . . . does this church present the New Testament, biblical view of money and stewardship? (2 Corinthians 9:7) *Let each one do just as he has purposed in his heart; not grudgingly or under compulsion . . .*

- T = *Teach* . . . will this church let *you* teach? This is very important. It's a great privilege to be able to lead a small-group Bible study, or Sunday school class, and contribute good Bible teaching to the church in this way. (Hebrews 5:12). . . . *by this time, you ought to be teachers* . . . It's also a great way to identify and invite one or two hungry ones in the group to meet for one-to-one discipleship and equipping. (2 Timothy 2:2) *The things you received from me in the presence of many witnesses, these entrust to faithful ones who can teach others also.*

It's rare that a solid local church restricts those it allows to lead a class or small group, but it does happen. One church I know which has a seminary of the same denomination near by, seems to permit only seminary students or professors to teach in the church. In another instance, from the best intentions perhaps, another church requires any teacher to be a member for at least five years, and requires teachers to adhere only to the curriculum specified by the pastor. The good intention here is possibly to protect the congregation from false teaching, but it still seems excessive and even a bit wary of a lay person's ability to teach doctrine as guided by the Holy Spirit.

Having found a good church, volunteer to lead a small group Bible study.

Most good churches welcome Bible study leaders. We'll assume your local church is confident in you to be a biblically accurate and qualified group leader. The church leadership may ask you to take over an existing group, or to start a new one. How do you know what kind of small group to invest in? The discussion that follows may seem harsh or non-inclusive, but we must be realistic concerning how to conduct a ministry that will contribute the most to God's Kingdom.

If your church asks you to take over the leadership of an *existing* small group, and you have a choice about which group to be involved with, keep your ministry goals in mind. Since your desire is to teach the whole group, but select and disciple a few, that should be the major factor in determining which group to volunteer to lead. For example, while older church members often exemplify godliness and commitment to prayer, they are *usually* not the most able to adapt to the activities or spiritual disciplines of discipleship. This is a generalization to which there are many exceptions. And the Holy Spirit will guide you to those into whom you can fruitfully impart your life, regardless of age or life situation.

For the sake of this discussion, however, we'll primarily consider young adults, or young couples (in their 20's). They have the energy, relatively few major life problems, and motivation to consider paying the cost of growing to maturity in the Christian faith.

If the church asks you to begin a new small group, you can recruit to this same constituency simply by specifying the age group and focus of the group. For example, an e-vite on the church website:

"New Bible study group for the 18 – 30's!
College students, alums, young adults, couples . . . all welcome!
Focus of the Bible study group: "Maturity in Christ!"
Studying key Bible passages and topics that help us grow and serve.
Led by Jacob Smith
Contact Pastor Jeremy if you're interested."

It's helpful, by the way, to have the assistant pastor, or small-groups pastor, be the contact person instead of you, as people will feel more comfortable signing up through a church staff member.

The ideal size of a small-group Bible study is about 8 – 10. This promotes good interaction and it means you can have the get-togethers pretty much anywhere, at the church or in a home. One of the main reasons people like small-group Bible studies is to have friends. A group of about this size is perfect for building friendships with other Christians that provide encouragement and accountability.

So, let's assume 10 people sign up for your small group. It meets weekly at your home. (By the way, snacks and drinks are good, but don't get too elaborate.) You have an initial get-together so people can start to build relationships. Give the group a hand-out briefly describing the topics you'll be studying for the first seven meetings. Make sure these topics are relevant to the group. Best bet is to have something like, e.g."Seven Hot Topics for Millennials!" These topics can discuss what the Bible says about relationships, resolving conflicts, knowing God's will for your life, money issues, etc. These are topics of sure-fire interest for most people, but especially the 20's age bracket.

Now begin leading the group! See *Question 2: How do I lead a small group Bible study?* for lots of suggestions on how to do this.

Pick a faithful one or two. As you meet week after week, keep your eyes open for those in the group who seem most interested, motivated, and hungry. This is pretty obvious, but you can have a few criteria in mind, such as . . .

- . . . persons who are attentive and engaged in the study as opposed to the one who's yawning and checking his watch . . . well, it might not be *that* obvious . . . but it's still quite clear who's interested in the Bible study and who's not.
- . . . those who ask good questions. Good questions indicate a person who is processing the concepts of the topic or passage and trying to dig deeper.
- . . . the person who takes the application of the Bible study seriously.

Let's say the group has just studied how to share Christ, having gone through John 4, Jesus talking with the woman at the well. You could throw out a bit of a challenge to the group sometime, such as, "I'm going over to the campus this Wednesday evening and just talk to some students about faith; anybody want to join me? You don't have to say or do a thing; just come with me." If someone volunteers to go with you, that's an excellent sign of a serious, growing young believer. Even if no one volunteers, it'll be pretty evident which ones at least wrestle with saying yes.

Overall idea here is to look for and identify the one or two in the group who would respond well to an offer from you to meet together for some discipleship and ministry training.

Help that person(s) to grow. Spend personal time with him or her.

Okay, let's assume you've identified a person you think is serious and interested in growing. Ask him / her if she / he would like to meet once a week. It's fairly easy to schedule this if the person is a college student, as students have lots of open spaces in their week. It's more difficult with folks who have jobs, especially if she / he has a family. It may have to be an early morning meeting, or a lunch near their workplace. Evenings are usually more difficult for a married person or one with a family, as that's the time of day when family is a priority.

Now that you've agreed upon a time and place, for example, lunch at the fast food place near the person's office, the big question then arises: "What do I do with this person?! How do I impart my life to her or him?" You can do with this interested young Christian what Paul did with his young man, Timothy.

It's been said that all ministry is essentially two things: love and truth. The best picture of this in the Bible (I think) is seen in 1 Thessalonians 2:7 & 11. Paul tells the believers in Thessalonica that he and his team were . . . *as a nursing mother tenderly cares for her own children.* (2:7) and . . . *how we were exhorting and encouraging and imploring each one of you, as a father would his own children.* (2:11) The loving heart of the mother and the exhorting, teaching heart of the father are good depictions of personal ministry. Anyone who has ever seen a mother with a baby or toddler knows what demonstrated and verbalized love looks (and sounds) like. In discipleship, it's affirmation of the younger Christian you're helping, and genuine praise. This is not pretense or flattery, but sincere appreciation for the person. Someone once said, "I can live a month on a good compliment!"

This heart of the mother builds trust in the relationship. The young Christian will come to see that you really do like him and care about him. He or she will feel, rightly so, that you are on her side.

The father's heart to teach and exhort is the "truth" part of this spiritual "Velcro." Paul describes his goal in ministering to the Colossian church this way:

> *...admonishing every man and teaching every man with all wisdom, that we may present every man complete in Christ.* (Colossians 1:28)

Helping someone else to grow is basically helping her or him to *do* and *be* what you do and are. As the Apostle Paul urged the believers in Philippi, *The things you have learned and received and heard and seen in me, practice these things; and the God of peace shall be with you.* (Philippians 4:9)

Christian disciplines which you know to be biblical—and that provide the foundation for your relationship with God—are the very same disciplines which another person will find foundational.

It's a simple idea—a kind of spiritual parenting—but it's one that's sometimes overlooked. Some may feel that personal, one-to-one ministry is just too slow or even inefficient. One man said to me, "It's too much attention given to too few people. If it's good training, why not give it to the biggest group you can?" While I understand this thinking, I feel there are some real strengths to personal discipleship.

- First, in this day when many young people struggle with a good self esteem, personal ministry demonstrates to someone that she or he is valuable. "If this Christian leader is spending personal time with me, he must think I'm worth it!" As the Apostle Paul put it, *...we were well-pleased to impart to you...our own lives, because you had become very dear to us.* (I Thessalonians 2:8) It has to do with the worth of the individual . . . the concept that individuals are *worth* receiving personal, one-to-one ministry, and that individuals are *worthy* of giving this kind of help to others.

- Second, one-to-one ministry is a great way to teach principles of life, character, and ministry because the instruction, feedback, and application can be tailored to the individual. It's an answer to the old criticism of group instruction that… "Telling isn't teaching; listening isn't learning!"

- Third, life-to-life ministry can result in spiritual multiplication, a kind of chain-reaction of lives impacting others for the Kingdom. Paul implied four generations of godly people when he said to Timothy… (Paul, Timothy, faithful ones, others) *You therefore, my son, be strong in the grace that is in Christ Jesus. And the things which you have heard from me in the presence of many witnesses, these entrust to faithful men, who will be able to teach others also.* (2 Timothy 2:1,2)

What "things" did Timothy learn from Paul? I'm sure there were a multitude of lessons and issues Timothy received from Paul during their time together, but let's look at a few key "things" mentioned in Paul's two letters to Timothy.

1. prayer –*Therefore I want the men in every place to pray* . . . (1 Timothy 2:8)

2. exhortation and teaching – *In pointing out these things to the brethren, you will be a good servant of Christ Jesus . . . give attention to the public reading of Scripture, to exhortation and teaching.* (1 Timothy 4:6,13)

3. time in the Word of God –. . . *and that from childhood you have known the sacred writings which are able to give you the wisdom that leads to salvation through faith which is in Christ Jesus. All Scripture is inspired by God and profitable for teaching, for reproof, for correction, for training in righteousness; that the man of God may be adequate, equipped for every good work.* (2 Timothy 3:15 –17)

4. sharing the Gospel –*I solemnly charge you in the presence of God and of Christ Jesus . . . preach the word; be ready in season and out of season; reprove, rebuke, exhort with great patience and instruction . . . do the work of an evangelist, fulfill your ministry.* (2 Timothy 4:1,2 & 5)

5. godly character – *Let no one look down on your youthfulness, but rather in speech, conduct, love, faith and purity, show yourself an example of those who believe.* (1 Timothy 4:12) Godly character has these three foundation stones:

   - sexual purity – (relate to) . . . *the younger women as sisters, in all purity.* (1 Timothy 5:2)

   - having God's perspective on money –*For the love of money is a root of all sorts of evil, and some by longing for it have wandered away from the faith* . . . (1 Timothy 6:7-11)

   - humility . . . seeing ourselves as God sees us, beloved and valuable; but not a self-made superman or superwoman . . . *not to think more highly of himself than he ought to think* . . . (Romans 12:3)

And let me add this, not mentioned explicitly by Paul in his letters to Timothy, but implicit in Paul's writing, and emphasized by Jesus:

friendships with other serious Christian men and women. These relationships are important for encouragement and accountability. I would use the term "fellowship," but that word has become so trite and misused as to mean little more than socializing.

Help the younger Christian to have these disciplines in his / her life (prayer, time in the Word, sharing the Gospel, teaching others). The basic approach to helping the younger believer is for you to share with him how you do it. Remember the saying, "You teach what you *know*; you reproduce what you *are*." In this relationship you have with a hungry-to-grow young Christian, you're providing both: your knowledge of Scripture and your own life as a model. Godly habits are more caught than taught. The Apostle Paul said numerous times that young believers should imitate him and his walk with God. This isn't pride or vanity. It's just common sense. People often emulate their leaders, which is beneficial when the leaders are living for God.

> *Imitate me as I imitate the Lord.* (1 Corinthians 11:1)

Now, train the young disciple for service to Christ. Jesus sent His disciples out (Luke 10:1–17) to experience ministry without Him. You encourage your ministry trainee to do same . . . lead his or her own small group, ID a hungry one, teach her or him these same disciplines that lead to a good walk with God. Discipleship is really just having someone do what you do, and equipping is just one more step beyond, having your disciple do the same for another. Aha! That's the very essence of 2 Timothy 2:2! Entrust good stuff to faithful ones who are able to teach others as well.

Conclusion: *You* walk with the Lord, and help other faithful ones to do the same. This is ministry.

(* For an in-depth look at how to disciple another, please see *Seven Principles of Ministry for the Average, Radical Christian*, Cunneen, Resource Publications, Eugene, Oregon, 2011, Chapter 3, pp. 13ff)

Question 2

How do I know what kind of ministry God is calling me to?

JUST AS THERE ARE different gifts and functions in the Body of Christ, there are different kinds of ministries. *There are varieties of ministries, but the same Lord.* (1 Corinthians 12:5)

Here are just some of the kinds of ministries we would recognize today:

- Evangelism
    - large group evangelism
    - one-to-one relational evangelism
    - cross-cultural evangelism
    - campus ministry evangelism
- Ministry to young children
- Ministry to people at the end of their lives (e.g. in nursing homes, assisted living facilities)
- Ministry to the afflicted or hurting . . . i.e. counseling
- Ministry to teens
- Ministry to families, focusing on family needs
- Discipleship
- Inner city ministry
- Foreign missions
- Ministry to those with addictions

- Financial counseling ministry
- Humanitarian aid ministry
- Pastoral ministry, i.e. shepherding people in the church
- Ministry to other religions or cults
- Seminary teaching
- Sunday school teaching
- ... others ...

How do I determine in which type of ministry God would like me involved?

Let me use a simple diagram to illustrate how we can narrow the choices down.

What God Calls Us To

Salvation	Growth To Maturity	Ministry	Kind of Ministry	Group to reach	Team to be part of	Where to do it
"...as many as received Him"	"...go on to maturity"	"...each use gift to serve"	"...there are variety of ministries"	"...chosen to bear My name to ..."	"... to be with Him"	"... to all "nations"

The three segments of the left – salvation, growth to maturity, ministry ... are what God says He desires for all persons. The four segments to the right represent the different kinds of ministry people can be involved in, the people-group that will be ministered to, the team a minister would be a part of, and the place (or location) where that ministry will take place. Here's an overview of each segment.

- *Salvation:*
    - Whom does God desire to be saved? ... *not wishing for any to perish but for all to come to repentance.* (2 Peter 3:9)
    - How is this determined; who gets saved? *But as many as received Him, He gave the right to become children of God, even to those who believe in His name.* (John 1:12)
- *Growth to maturity:*

- Whom does God desire to grow to maturity in their faith? *And we proclaim Him, admonishing every man, and teaching every man with all wisdom, that we may present every man complete in Christ.* (Colossians 1:28)

- How is this determined; who grows in faith? *And He was saying to them all, 'If anyone wishes to come after Me, let him deny himself, and take up his cross daily, and follow me.'* (Luke 9:23) People can choose to grow, or turn away; it's their choice.

• *Ministry:*

- Whom does God desire to minister? *Each one should use whatever gift he has received to serve others, faithfully administering God's grace in its various forms.* (1 Peter 4:10 NIV)

- How is this determined; who does ministry? *. . . but I chose you, and appointed you, that you should go and bear fruit, and that your fruit should remain . . .* (John 15:16) God appoints and commissions, but people have to want to serve and choose to do so. *You became imitators of us and of the Lord . . . for the word of the Lord has sounded forth from you . . . in every place your faith toward God has gone forth . . .* (1 Thessalonians 1:6 & 8)

These young believers in Thessalonica "imitated" Paul by going out to different places and sharing God's word with many others, choosing to pay the cost of serving God joyfully.

• *Kind of ministry:*

- This is the key issue: to discover what kind of ministry would be most fruitful for me to be involved in. Once that's determined, the rest—group to minister to, team to be part of, and location—logically fall into place.

- *Therefore, brethren, be all the more diligent to make certain about His calling and choosing you . . .* (2 Peter 1:10)

- How is this determined . . . ? *He gave some as apostles, and some as prophets, and some as evangelists, and some as pastors and teachers, for the equipping of the saints for the work of service, to the building up of the body of Christ.* (Ephesians 4:11,12)

Though it may seem complicated to determine what kind of ministry God would like a person to be involved in, it really boils down to three main factors:

1. *gifts & abilities* – how God has gifted and equipped me . . .
2. *passion* – what do I love doing . . .
3. *vision* – what concept of ministry captivates my heart and mind.

In other words, what is that person's ministry strength, what does he or she love to do, and what's the kind of ministry that she or he sees as extremely valuable for God's kingdom.

First, regarding the aspect of gifts and abilities: an example of two different men with different sets of abilities is Paul and Peter. Paul was educated and from a cultured background (Philippians 3:4ff); Peter was a fisherman. While Peter was intelligent and possessed a powerful personality, he probably lacked the social graces and education to be highly effective in ministry to Greeks and Gentiles. Consider Peter's speech to Roman centurion, Cornelius et. al. in Acts 10: 28, *And he said to them, you yourselves know how unlawful it is for a man who is a Jew to associate with a foreigner or to visit him; and yet God has shone me that I should not call any man unholy or unclean."* Wow, what a rude approach to sharing the gospel!

In contrast, Paul in Acts 17:19ff, comes to a place filled with false idols, and says, graciously, *Men of Athens, I observe you are very religious in all respects."* (Acts 17:22), then proceeds to share the gospel from a metaphysical basis (verses 24–28). This episode reveals Paul's strengths and abilities in pagan and/or sophisticated ministry situations.

In fact, Christ's statement in Acts 9:15 about Paul's ministry "job description" is this: *But the Lord said to him* (Ananias of Damascus), *Go, for he is a chosen instrument of Mine, to bear My name before the Gentiles and kings and the sons of Israel.* Paul was gifted and equipped to multi-task.

Both Peter and Paul were men who loved the Lord with all their hearts, and served Him with their lives. But the kinds of ministry in which they served God were certainly different.

Secondly, while God may challenge us at times by putting us in ministry situations in which we really feel inadequate and uncomfortable—perhaps to stretch our character and increase our humility—God normally employs those who serve Him in the kind of ministry that brings them *joy*. In fact, joy is a major aspect of finding out one's gift. (See Question 10, part 1, "How do I know what my spiritual gift is?")

Thirdly, our call will be consistent with our *Vision*. By that I mean the kind of ministry that grabs us, and compels us. Take for example, a person convinced that working with young children would be a great investment for their futures as adult Christians. That conviction would motivate that person to focus on that kind of ministry, leading young ones to a childlike faith in Jesus, and helping them, appropriate to their age, to be pleasing to God. That's what is meant by a compelling vision for ministry.

For me, the ignition point was hearing Dawson Trotman's (founder *of The Navigators*) message "Born To Reproduce." The vision in this message was that if each serious Christian were to spend enough time to help another young, interested Christian grow in faith and obedience, then that person could do (and likely, *would* do) the same thing with another person. Then there would be two people walking closely with God and having both the heart and skills to serve the Lord. Then the two would become four, then eight, then 16, 32, 64, 125, 250, 500, 1000, then 2000, *ad infinitum*. It was the idea of spiritual multiplication that captured my heart.

It was the wonderful realization that an individual person could have a huge impact on the world for Christ and do it in everyday life. It was the concept that the same way the world got populated—by human reproduction—was the way we could take part in getting the gospel to every person. As someone once quipped, the only commandment that people ever really gladly obeyed was, "be fruitful and multiply."

To paraphrase Trotman's biographer, Betty Lee Skinner, Trotman felt that two things—personal discipline unto godliness and the spiritual power of reproducing lives—". . . were largely lacking in Christian work . . . " and that God wanted Trotman to focus on this kind of ministry. (* Skinner, *Daws,* p. 270)

As you can tell, I am very excited by this vision, and have been for many years. God has put it on my heart. This is the kind of intensity and passion you should feel about the type of ministry to which you believe God is calling you.

So what are some kinds of ministries that match well with what kinds of gifts?

Let's say your passion is to help persons with emotional issues or life problems. You find your gifting is in the area of mercy and compassion. You have empathy with and communicate well with those who are struggling. The type of ministry may well be one of Christian *counseling*.

If your gifting is to be a behind-the-scenes helper, finding real joy in making sure everything is set up perfectly, e.g. for the conference, you may be that extremely valuable person: a *servant* of God who loves to work for the Kingdom, seeing needs and meeting them in the Christian community.

What if you enjoy bringing order to chaos, and excel in keeping your church or ministry operating smoothly? Your gift may be *administration*, one of the most essential parts of modern-day ministry.

Or, you find that whenever a Christian activity requires someone to step up and take charge, people look to you, and you enjoy giving direction to groups or events. Your gift might well be *leadership*, and this is a key function for most Christian endeavors. You recognize that leadership is important, but you remember that leading as the Lord did means humility, servant-hood, and being an example . . . not a boss.

- *People group:* Obviously, the group of people to whom you will minister depends primarily on the type of ministry to which you feel called.
  - If discipleship, the logical group would be college-age, or young couples.
  - If counseling, with the ones struggling with life issues, regardless of age.
  - If evangelism, to the lost in the USA or overseas.
- *Team:* Very few of us operate well alone. Being on a team brings us encouragement, learning and sharing opportunities, and a real sense of working together toward a biblical goal. Here are some likely connections with teams that fit well with your calling:
  - For myself, with a focus on discipleship = the *Navigators* ministry was a perfect fit.
  - Someone strong in languages, = *Wycliffe Bible Translators*, or *Wycliffe Associates* would make a wonderful partnership.
  - Serving ministry = local church lay ministry team, *Young Life* club host.
  - Teacher = Sunday school board, church small group council, seminary faculty.
  - Counseling = almost any church staff, an independent practice, volunteering at a mental-health center or a Veterans hospital,

or community addictions counseling center, or perhaps even a prison-based ministry team.

- If administration, your church office staff, or the administrative staff of any of the non-profit Christian organizations.
- Or . . . you may be the initiator of your own team, building a nucleus of co-laborers around your passion and vision.

The team may change from time to time, but the type of ministry will probably not change.

- *Location – where to do it:* Whereas the type of ministry you are called to by God will probably not change, the location often does. A person, for example, who loves evangelism can do that ministry pretty much anywhere. She or he may begin in a local high school ministry and find himself in a foreign country a few years later. The Apostle Paul was certainly a man who had evangelism, disciple-making, and church-planting on his heart, and he did it all over the Mediterranean world. The locations he went to were basically determined by God's leading. (Acts 16:9,10) *And a vision appeared to Paul in the night: a certain man of Macedonia was standing and appealing to him, saying 'Come over to Macedonia and help us.' And when he had seen the vision, immediately we sought to go to Macedonia, concluding that God had called us to preach the gospel to them.'*

The old saying in ministry is, "Keep your hearts open and your bags packed."

God can well use your service of ministry in many places. Or He may have you stay and minister in the same location your whole life. He will call you as He desires. One final thought on this topic: that is, the question of whether or not God wishes you to be a full-time Christian worker. This might be as a pastor, church staff person, missionary, or para-church minister.

While there is probably no one simple answer to this, I feel that the adage of "*grow* into ministry, rather than *go* into ministry" can be helpful. In other words, being committed to and significantly involved in personal ministry as a lay person gives one a solid idea of whether he or she should do it as a full-time vocation.

Conclusion: Once you've determined what kind of ministry God is calling you to—based upon your gifts & abilities, what you love to do, and the vision God has put on your heart—then the group of people you'll minister to, and the team you'll minister with, becomes quite evident. Where you'll minister depends on need and opportunity.

And remember, regardless of the type of ministry you pursue, the commands of Christ to share the Gospel, help others grow (spiritual parenting), and show love to all . . . apply to all Christians.

Question 3

How do I lead a small-group Bible study?

THERE'S GOING TO BE a bonus on this one. That is, we'll look at how to *write* a good small-group Bible study, as well as how to *lead* one.

In our Christian experience, there're few things more satisfying and profitable than a good small-group Bible study . . . and perhaps few things more boring and frustrating than a bad one. We've probably all been in some of the latter category, and hopefully, some of the first.

So here are a few tips and concepts for writing and leading a good Bible study group.

First, a good Bible study must actually study the Bible, not just some book from the local book store *about* Christian issues, or whatever the latest fad is. There are also some good Bible study booklets with relevant questions that point us to Bible verses and passages.

Second, writing a good Bible study means selecting a passage or topic which has interest and application for the intended group. For example, a study on the biblical principles of child-rearing would be great for couples with young children, but less relevant for singles.

Third, the key to writing a good Bible study is for *you*—the writer—to consider the passage / topic carefully and *come up with good questions*. A small-group Bible study should never be a lecture or sermon by the leader. It should be an interactive discussion that results in self-discovery—by the group members— of Biblical truths that can be applied to real life.

Let's quickly go through preparing the small group Bible study based on your own study of the passage or topic. In one sense, all Bible study is topical, even when we're looking at a particular passage. By that I mean that as we go through a passage of Scripture—say James, chapter 1—we invariably note issues or mini-topics in the text. That's why the Bible writer wrote it. So as we work through the passage, we are really seeing issues the author brings up, and we are then asking questions about those issues.

Okay, let's say we're going to lead a Bible study on James 1:1–8. I'm going to use the NASB version.

> "James, a bond servant of God and of the Lord Jesus Christ, to the twelve tribes who are dispersed abroad, greetings. (2) Consider it all joy, my brethren, when you encounter various trials, (3) knowing that the testing of your faith produces endurance. (4) And let endurance have its perfect result, that you may be perfect and complete, lacking in nothing. (5) But if any of you lacks wisdom, let him ask of God, who gives to all men generously and without reproach, and it will be given to him. (6) But let him ask in faith without any doubting, for the one who doubts is like the surf of the sea driven and tossed by the wind. (7) For let not that man expect that he will receive anything from the Lord, (8) being a double-minded man, unstable in all his ways."

Please keep in mind that we're not trying to do a definitive theological exegesis of the passage. We're working to write a clear, accurate, applicable study to help people in our small group gain joy and victory in their daily lives.

As you get going on your Bible study preparation, it's enjoyable and helpful if you have another person from your small group join you during this preparation time. Discussing the Bible passage together has some huge benefits: it generates excitement as you and your friend think of other relevant verses and questions and it's great training for the other person in preparing the study and, later on, leading a small group of his/her own.

The key to leading a good Bible study is to prepare well and write good questions. Guide, but don't monopolize, the discussion. So before we come up with a good Bible study on this passage, let me suggest 3 "do's" and 4 "don't's" to keep in mind about leading a small group Bible study:

Do's

Do a good Bible study on this passage yourself. If you do the work of really going through and thinking about a passage of Scripture, *you* will be excited about the Scripture, and this excitement will communicate to your small group. If you rely on, for example, a booklet from the local Christian bookstore that someone else has written, you defeat the purpose of "self-discovery" for yourself and the others in the group. True enough, there are some excellent Bible study helps available, but your excitement about the Bible study that you have personally done increases the probability *they* will actually study the Word for themselves. I have observed too often Bible study groups who go year after year "re-chewing" what *someone else* encountered in God's word. This gets pretty old after a while.

Do come up with some good thought-provoking questions which will generate discussion, then have some "follow-up" questions to guide the discussion.

Do have a clear, applicable conclusion. Yes, we want the small group to interact and discuss the topic, but the leader can and should give a brief, concise summation at the end of the study. The conclusion could suggest a few possible applications for people to consider. We'll see how this sounds as we go through a hypothetical Bible study.

Do Not's

Don't you talk too much! Nothing kills a good discussion faster and more fatally than the leader monopolizing the conversation. Sadly, this is an all-too-common problem in small groups. What should be a great opportunity to interact and hear others' views can become just another 40 minute sermon. I used to somewhat facetiously recommend the 17% rule for leaders; that is, if the whole group meeting were recorded, the leader's voice would not be heard more than 17% of the time.

Don't ask obvious or "yes/no" questions. This takes a little thinking about. There's an old joke about the little boy in a Sunday school class whose teacher asked questions to which the answer was usually "Jesus," as in "Who loves you the most?" Well, one day, the teacher said, "Okay, kids, what has a bushy tail, lives in a tree, chatters, and eats nuts?" The little boy said, "Well, it sounds like a squirrel, but I know it's Jesus." The point is, if your questions are too simple or obvious, discussion will quickly die.

Don't pick too many topics for a 40 minute Bible study. Limit the scope of the Bible study to one key topic—or at most two, related, topics—and concentrate on that. And by the way, stick ferociously to the 40 minute time limit. It's far better to have people leave a little hungry than stuffed. Plus, it's so unusual to end anything on time, that the novelty alone will be pleasing.

Don't have surprise, or mysterious, conclusions to your study.

Surprise twist endings are great for Agatha Christie mysteries, but not for Bible studies. Interest in the topic is generated by the truth itself, and the application to our lives, not by a tricky revelation at the end of the Bible study.

Doing the Bible study on James 1:1–8

Verse 1 – *James . . . to the twelve tribes who are dispersed abroad . . .* Okay, it would be an interesting study to investigate who this "James" is, why the "twelve tribes" are dispersed, and where . . . but probably not for a typical Bible study group. Save an intensive study of these issues for your own Bible study, or for a paper for a seminary class you may be taking.

Verse 2 – Now we've come to a applicable statement: *Consider it all joy, my brethren, when you encounter various trials . . .* What questions can you ask about this statement?

What kind of trials do people encounter?

How can people be joyful when difficult things happen?

Is this some special kind of joy? Different from happiness?

Will Christians *pretend* to be joyful with trials even if they're not?

Is this phony?

Verses 3, ... *knowing that the testing of your faith produces endurance. And let endurance have its perfect result, that you may be perfect and complete, lacking in nothing.*

Questions:

How do trials test our faith?

What does endurance have to do with our faith, or facing trials?

What in the world does that last part mean?? That endurance's result is that we might be perfect and complete?

Verse 5 – *But if any of you lacks wisdom, let him ask of God, who gives to all men generously, and without reproach, and it will be given to him.* Questions:

Is this lack of wisdom related to the trials? That is, are we asking God for an understanding of what the trial is about? For example, "Lord, please help me understand why I always seem to get passed over for promotion at work."

Why are we assured by James that God won't reproach us for asking for wisdom? Why would He? Seems like He sure got angry with Job for asking why all his (Job's) trials were happening. (Job 38:1,2)

Verses 6,7,8 – *But let him ask in faith without any doubting, for the one who doubts is like the surf of the sea driven and tossed by the wind. For let not that man expect that he will receive anything from the Lord, being a double-minded man, unstable in all his ways.* Questions:

What does it mean to ask without doubting?

Is "asking without doubting" the same as being sure that God will

give me wisdom about the issue I'm asking about? What if He doesn't? Does this mean I'm weak in faith?

What's the *nature* of this kind of doubting?

What does it mean to be "double-minded"?

What does it mean to be "unstable in all his ways"?

Now we have a good feel for the passage, and quite a few questions that will help the group discuss and discover applicable truth. Please realize that we can't possibly discuss and answer *all* the questions we've thought of. We'll pick a few key questions and focus our attention on them.

The next step is to see what other verses there are in the Bible that are relevant to this James passage.

Here are a few key questions we'll ask in the Bible study group. Other verses on this topic (cross references) can be easily found if your Bible has a small-print cross-reference index in the middle column or side margins.

What kind of trials did the early Christians face? How about today? In the first century: the book of Acts gives many instances of the early believers going through trials, including . . .

- Intimidation – (Acts 4:18) *And when they had summoned them, they commanded them not to speak or teach at all in the name of Jesus.* (Acts 4:18)
- Physical beatings –. . . *after calling the apostles in, they flogged them and ordered them to speak no more in the name of Jesus . . .* (Acts 5:40)

- Death – *And they went on stoning Stephen as he called upon the Lord and said, "Lord Jesus receive my spirit!"* (Acts 7: 59)
- Persecution of many believers –. . . . *great persecution arose against the church . . . Saul began ravaging the church, entering house after house; and dragging off men and women he would put them in prison.* (Acts 8:1,3)

The list of hardships and suffering goes on at length in Acts. The Apostle Paul's hardships and torments are frequent and serious. These are alluded to in Paul's letters to the Corinthian church. You can read his comments in 2 Corinthians 4:8–17; and 2 Corinthians 11:23–30.

What kind of trials do Christians face today?

- Health issues
- Family issues
- Money or job-related problems
- Others . . . ?

How can we be joyful at these times? And why? Here are some powerful verses that help us understand this seemingly difficult question:

. . . they rejoiced they had been considered worthy to suffer shame for His name. (Acts 5:41)

All discipline (from God) for the moment seems not to be joyful, but sorrowful; yet to those who have been trained by it, afterwards it yields the peaceful fruit of righteousness. (Hebrews 12:11)

. . . And we know that God causes all things to work together for good to those who love God and are called according to His purpose. (Romans 8:28)

How does testing improve our faith?

> *In this you greatly rejoice, even though now for a little while, if necessary, you have been distressed by various trials, that the proof of your faith, being more precious than gold which is perishable, even though tested by fire, may be found to result in praise and glory and honor at the revelation of Jesus Christ.* (1 Peter 1:6,7)

What kind of doubting is bad, and how do we avoid it?

> *And a leper came to Him, beseeching Him, and falling on his knees before Him, and saying to Him, "If You are willing, You can make*

me clean." And moved with compassion, He stretched out His hand, and touched him, and said to him, "I am willing; be cleansed" (Mark 1:40,41)

Compare this to the father in Mark 9:21–24

(Jesus). . . asked the father, "How long has this been happening to him?" and he said, "From childhood. And it has often thrown him both into the fire and into the water to destroy him. But if You can do anything, take pity on us, and help us!" And Jesus said to him, "If You can! All things are possible to him who believes" Immediately the boy's father cried out and began saying, "I do believe; help my unbelief."

The difference between the man in Mark 1 and the father in Mark 9 is captured in the two phrases: "if You are *willing*," and "if You *can*." The first man has faith Jesus can if He will. The second man seems to question *if* Jesus can do the miracle. This is why, I believe, Jesus answers the poor father almost sarcastically . . . "If *I* can!". . . meaning, "The issue here isn't whether I can, but whether you believe I can." Then the father cries out "help my unbelief." So when we ask God for His wisdom, we may ask if He is willing to impart wisdom, but not doubt that He can.

Another aspect of doubting would be a sort of "ask-God-as-a-last-resort" attitude that, "Oh, well, I might as well ask God for help or understanding. I've tried everything else, so I have nothing to lose." Let not that man think he will receive anything from the Lord!

Key: *And without faith it is impossible to please God, for anyone who comes to Him must believe that He exists, and that He rewards those who earnestly seek Him.* (Hebrews 11:6 NIV)

Conclusion to our brief Bible study on James 1: 1–8

James' teaching here assumes that all of us Christians are going to experience various trials, hardships, even suffering in our lives. We can be joyful because we know God is in control and that the difficulty can actually bring us increased strength as Christians. We can even ask God to help us understand the cause and/or resolution of the situation, and accept His response without doubting His ability to do what He knows is best for us.

Leading the Bible study group

You've done a good Bible study on the James 1 passage. Now let's see how you might lead this study with your small group.

The place you meet isn't particularly important; it could be a classroom at the church, or in someone's home. Of course, it's always good to have snacks, drinks, and that it's a relatively quiet location, without distractions, so people can enjoy fellowship.

Open with a brief prayer. Ask someone—not you— in the group to pray.

Then ask a fun question that everyone has to answer. For example, "If you could have a one-month, all-expenses-paid vacation anywhere on earth, where would you go?" Or, "what's the most unusual food you've ever eaten, and what was the circumstance?" Or, "What was the best Christmas gift you got as a kid?"

Why do we do this? It's an effective small-group dynamic to have each person in the group hear the sound of his or her own voice before the Bible study begins. This increases the possibility that people will contribute their thoughts during the Bible study. The more reserved people will be less shy about talking, and the more talkative people will be less likely to dominate the discussion because they've already listened to other voices.

If the group members don't know each other well, it's also good to have each person say her / his name during the fun question. Have everyone do this for several meetings. Why? It's quite common for people to be in a group—even for weeks— and not be sure about everyone's name. And after a certain period of time, people are embarrassed to admit they don't know someone's name and are afraid to ask. This can cause awkwardness in the group. I even have people say their middle names . . . there can be interesting stories related to middle names.

Have someone read the Bible passage the group is going to discuss. As a side note, find out in advance if there is anyone who hates to read aloud in a group.

Now ask your first "open-ended" general question to get the discussion going. This is a "long pause" question. That is, you ask the question, then wait . . . and wait and wait! In some small group settings, people are so used to the leader asking a question, then answering it himself in about 1/10th of a second, that it's a bit of a shock when the leader asks a question and actually expects people in the group to respond.

So when you ask a question, pause as long as it takes for someone to say something. Ha! This really can seem awkward when you first do it, but once the ice is broken, it goes really well, and people suddenly find themselves in an honest-to-goodness discussion. Then you can *guide* the discussion with follow-up questions. For example:

Opening question: "In the first few verses of James 1, the writer says Christians should "consider it all joy when we encounter various trials." What kind of trials do we encounter today?

Long pause. Finally, someone says, "Well, problems with raising kids . . ."

Then, after a much shorter pause, another person adds, "Money issues, as in not enough."

The hesitation fades away and more people jump in:

Kathy: " My washing machine broke down, and the store said the warrantee was worthless. "

Sean: " I got a really unfair grade in a stupid self-defense class! It lowered my GPA"

Greg: " I'm frustrated with my co-workers. I do most of the work but they share the credit. "

Laura: "I don't know why God would allow my nephew's leukemia to come back."

The point here is that the "various trials" that Christians struggle with, and seek wisdom on, can range from catastrophic situations to the tribulations of daily life.

At this point, you can ask follow-up questions that allow the group to explore the issue more deeply.

You: "How do you all think we can be *joyful* in these situations?" Again, allow people to answer.

(Hint: Keep your questions simple and brief, without qualifiers. For example, don't ask, "How do you think we can be joyful in these situations? Isn't that difficult? Is it reasonable?" These are valid questions, but don't bunch them all together, so that people aren't sure what question—of the 3—you're asking.)

Greg: "Well, the verses say that when faith is tested, it has a good result for us."

You: "Okay. What's the result?"

Moment of silence.

Then Laura (with a little attitude): "It mentions perseverance that results in Christians being mature. Then it says, not lacking anything. I don't know what that means."

You: "Anybody have an example of this?"

Kathy: "I think I do. My college roommate . . . etc."

This kind of interaction, based upon "unpacking" a Bible passage is, I believe, the most helpful way to have people in a small group gain understanding and benefit from the group meeting.

Keep it going in the same way. You ask questions, such as . . .

"Why do you think you might not receive wisdom from God about trials you're facing?"

"What kind of doubt do you think this passage is talking about?"

"Is it or isn't it natural to doubt we'll always get God's wisdom about things?"

"If you asked for wisdom about something and didn't feel you got God's wisdom, wouldn't that cause you to doubt the next time you ask for wisdom?"

At this time, you could introduce some helpful other verses (cross references) to clarify some of the questions.

"Would someone read Mark 9:21-24. And someone else read Mark 1:40,41 Do you all see any difference in these two interactions with Jesus?"

When the 40 minute time limit is almost up, you, the leader, give a brief conclusion.

"Let me share the 2 key points I got from this little study. First, it's a normal part of life to have problems and trials. We can respond to trials one of three ways: one, be overwhelmed by them and feel defeated when we face these situations; two, practice denial and ignore them as best we can, or three, realize that with God's strength and wisdom, we can actually grow in faith and spiritual strength *because* of the trials. This is, of course, what Romans 8:28 tells us, *All things work together for good to those who love the Lord and are called according to His purposes.* I call this the verse that everyone knows but finds hard to believe.

"And second, that we can ask God to help us understand the reason for the difficulty, or even how it's going to be resolved, trusting that God certainly can if He is willing to do so."

You: "Okay. Great discussion on this interesting and challenging passage. Any one have possible applications? What can we actually do to benefit from this?"

Greg: "Well, I've realized that even though I ask God for understanding a lot, I usually don't really think He's going to answer. So, I'm going to work on asking seriously, and be like the guy that said 'Help me in my unbelief.'"

Laura: "I'm going to try to stop being mad at God about my nephew. I still don't think I'm going to understand about the cancer, but I hate being angry at God."

Others share.

You: Laura, would you close our time with a word of prayer?

Laura prays.

End on time. Do not go long.

Better to have people leave a little unsatisfied and wanting more, than stuffed with too much and wondering—like Jonah in the belly of the fish—"Will I ever get out of here!?"

That's it. You can be a great leader of small group Bible studies. It is really a joy to be part of an interactive group. God's Word is "living and active" and will give peace, victory, and power to serve to those who apply it to their lives. Just remember these three essentials:

- Use the Bible as your text
- Ask good questions & let them self-discover. Don't *tell* them . . .
- Do not—I say again—do not talk too much!

Question 4

How do I share the gospel relationally?

Telling others about Jesus, many Christians think, is one of the scarier aspects of their faith. It does seem like an intimidating challenge . . . but really it's quite easy. Like fighting Goliath: scary, but easy because the target is so big. Those without a relationship with God through Christ are all around us. It's not at all like trying to locate the elusive Loch Ness monster. But we do have to deal with our feelings of nervousness or inadequacy.

So let's begin with three Biblical facts:

1. People are separated from God, now and eternally, because of their sin.. . . *your iniquities have made a separation between you and your God.* (Isaiah 59:2)

2. God has provided a way for people to be forgiven and enter into a relationship with God—Jesus Christ. *But God demonstrates his own love for us, in that while we were yet sinners, Christ died for us.* (Romans 5:8)

3. We Christians need to tell people about Christ so they can be saved. *. . . And how shall they believe in Him* (of) *whom they have not heard?* (Romans 10:14)

But there's a problem that hinders some Christians from sharing their faith: embarrassment! We may feel embarrassed to speak about Jesus Christ to our non-believing friends, family or co-workers because it's not "cool" or politically correct to be a person who believes in Jesus.

It may have been the same in the first century. Paul says in Romans 1:16 *I am not ashamed of the gospel; it is the power of God for salvation to everyone who believes* . . .

Why does Paul say, "I am not ashamed"? He might have mentioned "I am not fearful;" or "I am not unprepared."

Or the apostles, having been flogged for talking about Jesus . . . *went on their way from the presence of the Council, rejoicing that they had been considered worthy to suffer shame for His Name.* (Acts 5:41)

Or the exhortation in Hebrews 13:12,13 . . . *Jesus also, that He might sanctify the people through His own blood, suffered outside the gate* (i.e. holy place). *Hence, let us go out to Him outside the camp* (i.e. our comfort zone), *bearing His reproach* (shame).

Finally, there are the words of the Lord Jesus, concerning people's embarrassment: *For whoever is ashamed of Me and My words, of him will the Son of Man be ashamed when He comes in His glory* . . . (Luke 9:26)

Having determined, therefore, to not be ashamed of Jesus and His gospel, and willing to be viewed as "one of those religious people" in the eyes of the world, we can now consider the best way to tell others about salvation through Christ.

Let's use an illustration called *The Circle of Five*.

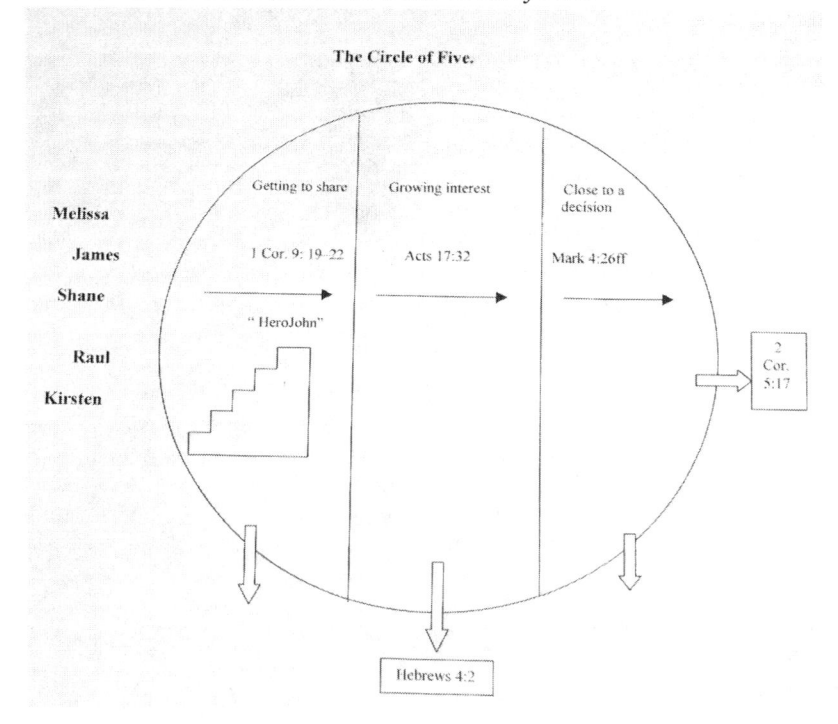

The Circle of Five.

Melissa
James
Shane
Raul
Kirsten

Getting to share — 1 Cor. 9: 19–22 — "HeroJohn"
Growing interest — Acts 17:32
Close to a decision — Mark 4:26ff

2 Cor. 5:17

Hebrews 4:2

The circle represents our own sphere of relationships with those who are not Christians, perhaps friends or family members. They're represented by the names on the left of the circle. Possibly you have a lot more non-Christian friends, but we'll just consider the five we feel are most open to "religion,"—as they might think of this. What we can pray for is the opportunity to share about Christ, then graciously help them to move toward a decision to receive God's offer of salvation through Christ.

So let's assume we're praying for, and trying to share with, the friends we see to the left of the circle above.

The three sections of this circle represent three stages (for lack of a better word) of you sharing the gospel and helping him or her come to a decision about Christ, either to accept Jesus as Savior or decide not to.

The section on the left, "Getting to share," and the 1 Corinthians 9 reference, simply represents our prayers and efforts to share the gospel. The little "staircase" (and "HeroJohn") you see depicts five natural steps to get to present the gospel. More about that a little later on.

The middle section, "Growing interest" describes a person's desire to know more about God and Jesus. This is not always the case, of course. As Acts 17:32 states, . . . *when they heard of the resurrection of the dead, some began to sneer, but others said, 'We shall hear you again concerning this.'* It's the ever-present truth: some sneer; others want to know more. So after you've shared the gospel with your friend, you can water and cultivate the seed that's been sown by maintaining the relationship, and keeping the conversation going. Just simple, polite questions such as "Have you had any more thoughts on that little illustration?," or "I thought your idea about God being loving was good. Have you always seen Him that way?" We don't want to be pushy. We just want to keep the matter on the front burner. It is the Holy Spirit who will convict and draw the person to God.

The section on the right, "Close to a decision," means that a time will come when we sense the person knows enough, i.e. has a clear idea of God's offer, and is at the point of making a decision about Christ. Mark 4:26–29 is an agricultural illustration that says a farmer's job is to sow seed and then harvest it. He doesn't know *how* the seed grows; he just recognizes when it's time to harvest. We too can recognize when the seed of the gospel has come to maturity, and we can gently bring the question up: "Would you like to believe in Christ?" This may sound a bit scary, but you and your friend have been talking about Jesus for a while, and he or she will not be either surprised or offended. One person said to me, "I wondered when you were going to ask that." He seemed hurt to think I might not care enough to ask.

The arrow leading out of the circle to the right to 2 Corinthians 5:17 is what we pray for: your friend has asked Jesus Christ to be his or her Savior. *If anyone is in Christ, he is a new creation . . .*

People can "vote out" of moving toward Christ at any time. That's what the downward pointing arrows indicate. . . . *but the word they heard did not profit them, because it was not united by faith in those who heard.* (Hebrews 4:2)

Okay, back to section one of the circle, how to get to share the gospel.

The Scripture mentioned, 1 Corinthians 9:19–22, is the passage in which Paul states his plan for reaching out to non-believers: *to bring people to Christ, go where they are.* I also title this passage, "How To Be a Godly Phony like Paul." No, Paul isn't really a phony, or dishonest, but he does relate closely to whatever group of people he's with. This isn't pretense; it's Paul personally identifying with different kinds of people in order to gain credibility, share the gospel meaningfully, and hopefully lead some to Christ. The idea is that if anyone is going to have to get out of his comfort zone, it'll be Paul, not those he's trying to reach.

> *For though I am free from all men,* (that is, Paul doesn't *have* to defer or pander to anyone) *I have made myself a slave to all* (he takes on the obligation of relating to others on their terms, not his) *that I might win the more. And to the Jews I became as a Jew, that I might win Jews; to those who are under the Law, as under the Law, that I might win those who are under the Law; to those who are without law, as without law, though not being without the law of God but under the law of Christ, that I might win those who are without law. To the weak I became weak, that I might win the weak; I have become all things to all men, that I may by all means save some.*

What a wonderful, freeing passage this is. It's freeing because we can rid ourselves of hyper-spiritualizing the idea of what our role is in evangelism . . . that "people don't win anyone to Christ; only God does that!" While it's true that it's not our power of persuasion that draws people to Christ, but the conviction of the Word and the Holy Spirit, Paul says "that *I* might win some . . . that *I* might save some . . ." Don't diminish the importance of the messenger, or the careful planning Paul put into trying to connect with, and win, people in these different groups.

What might be the modern-day equivalents of these groups: under the Law, without the law, the weak? And how would we "become as" them in order to relate and identify?

> Those under the Law – well, unless the group you are trying to reach is comprised of orthodox Jews, those under the law might more likely be defined as those persons who are legalistic in some fashion. These are folks who find a sense of security in adhering to a set of rules, of some kind, either religious rules or the rules of a particular sub-culture they relate to.

> Those without law – this is a far easier set of people to find. At least in the US culture, with an prevailing attitude of self-determination regarding morals and ethics, they are widespread and numerous. *In those days, there was no king in Israel; every man did what was right in his own eyes.* (Judges 17:6)

> The weak – the hurting, insecure, fearful, etc.

The key thought here is that we don't have to participate in sin to get close to the sinner. We as Christians can make an effort to understand the life situation of those we desire to share with, and relate to them accordingly. As one pastor put it, "In evangelism, if anyone's going to be uncomfortable, it's going to be me. Jesus went where the sinners were, and so am I!"

Let's consider now some practical steps to go from spiritual ground zero, to sharing the gospel. The following illustration is just a guide—and prayer stimulus—for moving toward a gracious presentation of Jesus Christ.

5 Steps to Get There...

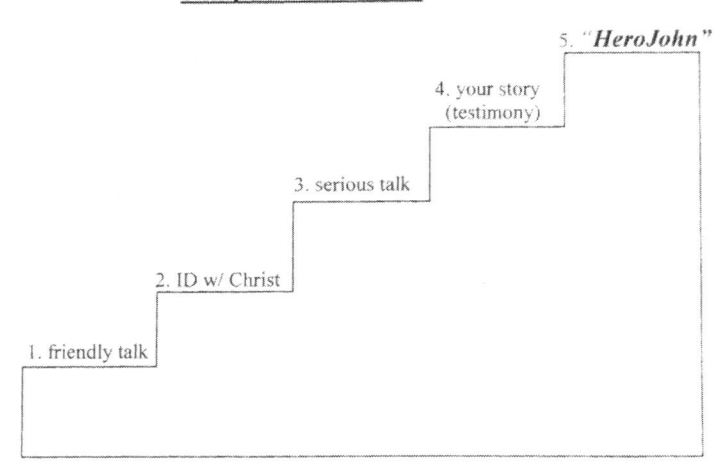

1. friendly talk
2. ID w/ Christ
3. serious talk
4. your story (testimony)
5. *"HeroJohn"*

Step 1 – Friendly talk . . . *I have become all things to all men* . . . (1 Corinthians 9:22) This first step comes pretty naturally. It's just us talking with a friend, or even new acquaintance, about superficial daily issues. Remember, we want to relate to him or her, and draw them out, on topics *they* find interesting.

Step 2 – ID with Christ. . . *I'm not ashamed of the Gospel...* (Romans 1:16) Step two is you identifying with Christ. All this really means is that your friend knows that you're a "religious" person. Then they won't be surprised when you bring the conservation around to spiritual matters. And please be cool about this. Don't say, "Just so you know, I'm a born-again, washed-in-the-blood-of-the-Lamb Christian!" You might mention in passing, "Oh, all the cars at the house on Tuesdays, that's a Bible study my wife and I have for some of the neighbors." That's really all it takes to let them know there's a spiritual element in your life.

Step 3 – Serious talk . . . *Men of Athens, I observe that you are very religious* . . . (Acts 17:22ff) Step three is shifting the conversation to more serious life topics. These often concern people's fears or anxieties. It may be about raising children, about relationships, about disappointments, or any other life issue that get beneath the surface of everyday life. In Acts 17, Paul makes the transition from complimenting those in Athens on their religious interest, to an explanation of God's nature and plan. We too can be aware of people's deeper life issues and make a transition to the Biblical perspective on these very issues. This step is probably the one most Christians find a bit intimidating. We may feel it's risky to shift to Bible perspectives, but remember, we've already identified with Christ, so people are not usually shocked at this.

Step 4 – Your story . . . Paul tells his story of how he became a Christian. A good way to relate to a non-Christian about serious life issues is to share some of your own spiritual journey. (Acts 26: 4-23) It may relate to a struggle you had, or even a joyful event that you didn't expect, but it should refer to how the Bible had good advice or answers to the situation you were in.

Step 5 – Share the gospel illustration: *"HeroJohn"* (See below how to do this illustration) *There is salvation in no one else* . . . (Acts 4:12) The last step is to ask, "Could I show you a little illustration that really helped me understand about God? I'd love to see what you think of it." Draw out the illustration fairly quickly, then ask them about any thoughts or questions they may have. The Bible promises us that when His word is shared, it is effective and does God's purposes, no matter how people respond.... *When My word goes out, it never comes back empty . . .it will accomplish My purpose* . . . (Isaiah 55:11) So don't worry about how your friend reacts to seeing the illustration. The seed has been planted.

One last thought about the five steps is "pray each step". That is, pray "God, please let me understand where my friend is in her life . . . " for step one. Then, for step two, pray "Lord, please help me come up with a good way to let my friend know I'm a Christian." Pray as you go along, specifically for each step of the journey. This keeps your prayers on target, not vague or generalized. It's also helpful to remind us to how many people we know that we can bring into our "circle of five." For instance, you may think, "There's five people I know at work that don't even know I'm a Christian . . . " and begin to pray step # 2 for them.

Let me give an example of these five steps. I go frequently to the local UPS store, and I'd been able to get to know Brian, the young man who worked there. Here's what I'd learned about Brian:

- He's 23 years old.
- He works long hours at the UPS store, but he likes his job.
- He lives in a one-bedroom apartment with three dogs he adopted from the pound.
- He doesn't have a girlfriend, which makes him sad.
- He doesn't curse; he feels using bad language is wrong.
- He collects old movies on DVD's, and he'd like to go to college and be a film major.
- He thinks I walk to the UPS store from "the church," because I don't park in the fire lane in front of the store.

I'd been praying for an opportunity to share the Gospel with Brian, following the little "5 step stair-case" plan. The friendly talk step is easy. Since I saw Brian frequently, I made a point of greeting him (unless he was busy serving customers!) and chatting. In this case, it was also quite easy for me to identify as being a Christian, since I come in to receive mail and packages for the ministry (*Life To Life Ministry*). Brian thought I worked for a nearby church; I don't (I work in college ministry), but that's okay; the key thing is that he knew I was "religious."

It was quite easy, as well, to talk with him on more serious topics, drawing Brian out on what he thought about life issues. And again, I was sensitive not to interfere with his work schedule in any way, but to talk with Brian during moments when nothing was happening in the store.

Here's a bit of how we got into the more serious topics.

Me: "Man, you must work a lot of hours; I see you here pretty much every time I come in."

Brian: "That's for sure. But I like lots of hours."

Me: "Well, that's different. Most people hate long hours."

Brian: (Laughs) "Not me. I like being in the store, plus I'm saving up for Valencia (local community college), and hopefully UCF."

Me: "Hey, that's great. What do you want to major in?"

Brian: "Definitely film. I love that stuff."

Me: "Bet your girlfriend doesn't like the long hours . . . " (This comment was a bit risky, but Brian didn't mind.)

Brian: "Don't have a girlfriend right now."

Me: "Ah . . . You're kidding! Good-looking guy like you?"

Brian: (very seriously) "Girls stress me . . . not sure why."

Me: "Ha! Well, you're not the only one."

Okay, I thought, the girlfriend issue was the serious topic we could discuss to lead to my being able to present the gospel to Brian. So at this point, I shared quickly about dating issues the students in the UCF Bible study wrestled with, and said the next time I came in, I'd tell him what the UCF guys and women had decided.

By the way, in trying to discover what life issues a non-Christian has, I don't judge or reprove any possible sin that may be involved. My goal is to share the good news of salvation in Christ, not rebuke a slave (to sin) for his chains.

The next time I saw him, I told him that the Bible had some great ideas about what made a really good guy-girl relationship. Brian looked puzzled, but was okay with me sharing relationship principles from the Bible and a verbal gospel message with him. If the setting were different, that is, not a workplace environment, I'd sketch out a little picture of the gospel based upon Romans 5:8—see below— but it can be done verbally as well.

A week after I'd talked with Brian about the gospel, he was gone. He'd been transferred to a UPS store on the other side of the city. I was sorry about not seeing him, but glad I'd had a chance to at least plant a seed of God's offer to people.

Jesus once told His disciples that they were reaping spiritual fruit where others had planted. Today, I feel, a lot of gospel-sharing is planting seeds, not reaping.

Did my little plan make Brian more of a project than a person? No; I really liked Brian, and enjoyed talking with him. Was my motive in getting to know him so I can win him to Christ? Yes. But I think that's okay. I believe it's what Paul had in mind in *I become all things to all men that by all possible means I might save some.* (1 Corinthians 9: 22)

While it's true that I'm being deliberate in trying to share Christ with him, it's not about having more notches on my evangelistic gun-belt, but just about looking for chances to tell people about Christ. It's really not difficult, but truthfully, a lot of times, being in a rush, I'd much rather zoom in and zoom out of the UPS store, not making an effort to get to know the people who work there. I think this is probably true for many of us. We want to share Christ, but our hectic schedules make it challenging to do. My prayer for all of us is that God would give us many opportunities to tell others about Jesus, our Savior and Lord.

"HeroJohn" gospel illustration

Let's go through how to share this with someone. We present this little illustration as simply as possible, drawing it out by hand on whatever paper is lying around. It may seem odd, but the less "professional" this gospel illustration is, the better.

Start by asking if you could draw out a little sketch that illustrates what the basic idea of Christianity is. I often say something like, "I'd like to show this to you and see what you think." This lets the person know that I respect his or her opinions and input. It communicates that I'm not going to preach at them or "guilt-trip" them.

The illustration:

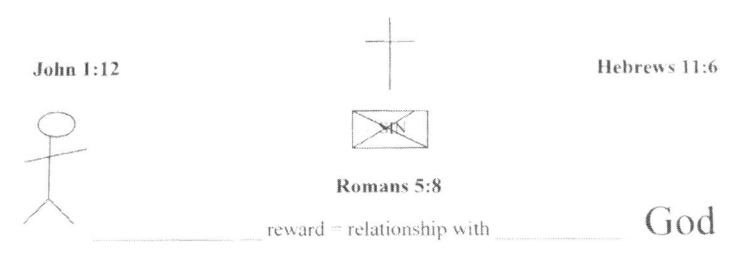

John 1:12   Hebrews 11:6

                        Romans 5:8
            reward − relationship with   God

"HeroJohn" just stands for He-Ro-John, Hebrews, Romans, John . . . as in Hebrews 11:6, Romans 5:8, and John 1:12.

Yeah, I know, that's pretty corny, but I need silly ways to remember illustrations.

Let me share the basic theology of this illustration, then I'll give an example of how it might look in a pretty typical interaction. This illustration begins on the right and moves left.

Point 1 is that God does exist and that He cares about people. He likes people to seek Him out, and rewards those who do.. . *For those who would draw near to God must believe that He exists, and that He rewards those who seek Him.* (Hebrews 11:6).

Point 2 is that God shows He cares about people by providing what people need most: forgiveness of sins because of Christ's sacrifice for us. Romans 5:8 *God demonstrates His love for us in that while we are yet sinning, Christ died for us.*

Point 3 is that people can have a relationship with God if they accept Christ. John 1:12 . . . *as many as received Him, to them He gave the right to become children of God . . .*

It's also helpful to have two other Scripture verses in mind to clarify this simple illustration: Romans 3:22,23 . . . *there is no distinction; for all have sinned and fall short of the glory of God* . . . This helps explain the Romans 5:8 statement that Christ died for us because of our sin; and 1 Peter 3:18 . . . *For Christ also died for sins, once for all, the just for the unjust, in order that He might bring us to God* . . . This statement explains the wonderful "substitution"—that Christ brought us to God by paying the price of death in our place.

By the way, I believe that paraphrasing verses of Scripture—as well as quoting an authorized version— retains the power of the Word if the paraphrase does not alter the essential meaning of the Scripture.

The following is an example of a conversation you might have with a non-believer as you share this gospel illustration. We'll say his or her name is "Alex," and you've built a good relationship so asking this question isn't uncomfortable.

You – "Okay if I draw out this little deal that gives the basic idea of what Christianity is about? I'd like to hear what you think."

Alex – "Sure . . . "

You – "My art work isn't great, but it's fast."

(Draw a stick figure person on the left, the word God on the right, and a line between the two.)

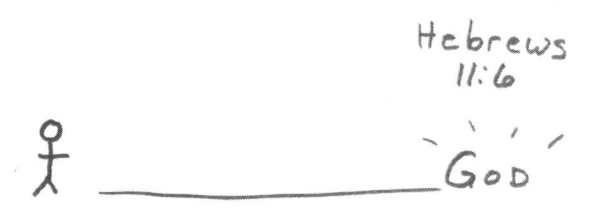

Hebrews 11:6

👤 ——————————— GOD

You – "So the general goal of religion is to answer the question, 'How do people connect with God?' There's a statement from the Bible—in a chapter called Hebrews, section 11 and statement 6— that says that people who are interested in coming toward God can be sure that He does really exist, that He cares about them, and rewards those who look for Him." (Here quote or paraphrase Hebrews 11:6) . . . *those who want to come to God must believe that He exists, and that He rewards those who seek Him* . . . Then ask, "The statement says God does exist. Would you say most of your friends believe in God, or not?" (By the way, we call Bible verses "statements" because it sounds less religious, or poetic. So, it's a *chapter* called Hebrews, *section* 11, *statement* 6)

Alex – "I don't really know, to be honest. We don't talk about religion. I guess maybe some of them do."

You – "Okay. Here's the second statement. It's from a chapter called Romans, and says that God proves that He cares about people by giving them the thing, or reward, they need the most to connect with Him. See if you see what that is. (Paraphrase or quote Romans 5:8) *God demonstrates His love for us in that while we were yet sinning, Christ dies for us. "*

Alex – Whoa! That's a big jump. How'd we get from God existing to Christ dying and us sinning?"

You – "Yeah, that's a lot of issues. "Sin" is kind of a religious term, but the concept is that the biggest problem we have getting to God, is that everybody does selfish, wrong stuff. (This is the paraphrase of Romans 3:23) Would you agree with that?"

Alex – Nobody's perfect."

You – "Exactly. And it's not just mistakes we make, but things that we know are wrong or hurtful, and we do them anyway, like deliberately. So if we went into God's presence the way we are, we'd pollute Him. But He still cares about us and wants to have a relationship with us."

(Here draw in a little box with the word "sin" in it, then put an X over it to depict that Christ has cancelled out the sin. Draw a cross over the box.)

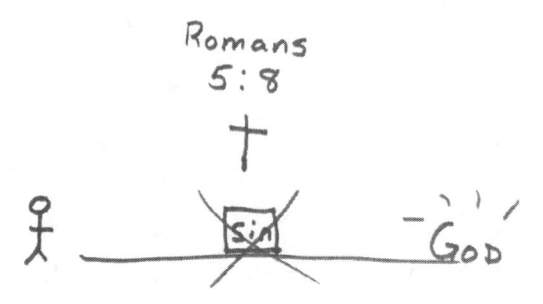

Romans 5:8

[diagram: stick figure ——— [sin with X] ——— God, with cross above]

You - (State this, but don't dwell on it, or use "church words.") "I know there's no way in a million years I'd ever get perfect enough to be with God. That's the reason God himself, that is, Christ, has to pay the penalty for our bad actions. (This is the paraphrase of 1 Peter 3:18) Another statement just says Christ died for our wrongs to bring us to God. Does that make sense?"

Alex – "Yeah, I see the logic. Seems harsh though. Christ dying for some petty selfish thing I do . . . "

(Note: if your friend shifts from the hypothetical to himself, or herself, like Alex did here, this is very good!)

You – "Yes, it sure does! Well, God sees any sin as being like cancer. Alex, you seem like a really good person, way better than most, but you don't have to have many cancer cells for to it kill you eventually. It's not like all the good cells balance out the cancer cells.

Alex – Ah . . . okay. Is that it?"

You – One more statement. (Quote or paraphrase John 1:12 . . . *as many as received Him, to them he gave the right to become children of God* . . . "All this says is that everybody has to make a decision whether he wants a relationship with God or not. If I want that, and accept what Christ has done, then God says I have a relationship with Him."

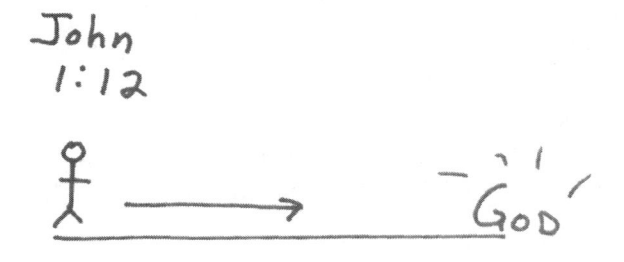

John 1:12

[diagram: stick figure ——→ God]

You – "Does this make sense?"

Alex – "It makes sense. I'll have to think more about it."

Go into as much discussion as the person wants to, but try to get through the illustration as quickly as possible. If too many side issues come in, it can muddy up the simplicity of the gospel message.

Ask as many questions as you can, and listen carefully to the answers. This helps the person hearing the gospel to not dismiss the points of the gospel as *your* opinion. See Question 5 for some hard questions non-Christians might ask.

That's it. Sometimes I'll ask in a friendly way, "Where do you think you are on this illustration? Trying to draw near? Not interested? Not sure? The great thing, I believe, is that people who are trying to find out if God exists, or how to connect with Him, He definitely wants to be found. God is not an elitist."

And remember, no matter how your friend or family member responds, you've planted the seed of life. Now it's up to the Holy Spirit and the person's heart response.

Question 5:

What are tough issues non-Christians bring up?

Our purpose in responding to the questions non-Christians ask is not to win arguments. It's to present biblical truth as clearly and politely as possible. . . . *always be prepared to give an answer to everyone who asks you to give the reason for the hope that you have. But do this with gentleness and respect* . . . (1 Peter 3:15 NIV)

These quick responses are certainly not theologically complete. The answers are just so you can have a true and gracious reply to legitimate questions non-believers may have, without sounding preachy or defensive. My experience is that those who are not Christians don't really want to hear long, comprehensive explanations to their questions anyway. The interactions tend to be brief, even with family members or friends. These suggested responses, therefore, are quick and to the point and, hopefully, biblical. Don't worry about how people react to your answers. If your responses to tough questions are gracious (not argumentative) and Scriptural, the job of convicting hearts is up to the Holy Spirit, not our power of persuasion.

We'll look at key verses and concepts before each one of these, but then I'll present them in dialogs to give an idea of how such conversations might go.

Here are the top 3 tough issues:

- First tough question: *If God is loving, why is there so much evil and pain in the world? Why doesn't God prevent it?*

    Key concept: God created man and woman to be in intimate, deep relationship with Him. An essential part of this relationship is that people *have to be* choice-makers. Without being able to choose

What are tough issues non-Christians bring up?

whether to enter into a relationship with God—or for that matter, any other person—the nature of the relationship would be superficial and meaningless. This is probably why God put a "forbidden" tree in the Garden of Eden. While it's certainly true that Eve and Adam made the wrong choice, it was important that they *had* a choice.

The consequences of that wrong choice have affected all mankind, and the fallen world is, to some degree, characterized by sin, disease, and evil. This is reality. An aspect of the pain in the world is disease (both physical and mental), and the consequences of people choosing to sin, often against others.

Key verses: Romans 1: 28,29 accurately describes God's permission of sin and disease in this earthly existence. You can paraphrase or quote these two verses as you talk with a questioner . . . but basically the gist is that God allows sin and evil to take place because it is consistent with His creation of mankind, and His plan of salvation. And we Christians also know that God is still in control (as He was in Job's ordeal), and that for believers . . . *all things work together for good to those who love God and are called according to His purpose.* (Romans 8:28) In fact, many believers testify that it was the hard, painful things in life that caused them to seek—not blame—God.

So, your friend asks the question. You answer, saying, "Good question. If I hear you right, you're saying that the fact there's evil and suffering, even to innocent people, and God doesn't stop it, it's because He's either uncaring or powerless. Right?"

"Exactly. If my little boy was going to run out in the road and get hit, and I could stop him, but didn't, I wouldn't be much of a dad."

"Yeah, good analogy. And I agree with you 100% that if God can't prevent bad stuff, or doesn't really care that it happens, I wouldn't believe in that kind of "god" either."

"So what's the answer?"

"Well, let me throw another factor in here. I mean, other than if He's uncaring or limited in what He can do. It's the free will factor."

"How's that explain God's inaction?"

You ask, "Can I read you one interesting Bible section, and see what you think it means?"

Your friend groans, but nods. "This isn't some 'just believe' stuff, is it?"

"No. Actually, it's more philosophical than anything. Anyway, it's the first section of the chapter titled Romans. It says,

And just as people did not see fit to acknowledge God any longer, God gave them over to a depraved mind, to do those things which are not proper, being filled with all unrighteousness, wickedness, greed, evil; full of envy, murder, strife, deceit, malice . . . (Romans 1:28,29)

"So, what do you think it means, 'God gave them over' to depravity and evil?"

Your friend replies with his own question. "Are you saying that 'gave them over' means he could do something but doesn't? What, is he just ticked off at mankind so he lets them do whatever they want? How is that good!"

You – "Well, God's sure honoring people's free will, even to do wrong actions. Can you think of how God letting people choose is a positive thing?"

"Honestly, no."

"Okay, here's the philosophical part, or maybe it's really more like psychology. I think God gives people free will, or choice—even for evil—because if they didn't have choice, they'd be little more than programmed computers, or squirrels, or whatever. Anyhow, the reason God created people was to have a deep, significant relationship with Him. That means they get to choose whether they want that or not."

"Whoa . . . there's a lot more to mankind than free will."

"True, but without free will, their ability to have a real relationship with God—or anybody for that matter—is diminished. It'd be shallow and pretty one-sided. Like if your wife *had* to marry you; you'd never know if she loved you or not. The fact that she chose you has huge meaning."

Your friend says, "You really think free will is that important?"

"Sure. Even the angels had free will. A lot of them used it to rebel . . . well, that's another story.

"Anyway, my reason for God allowing bad things to happen is that He'll never violate a person's choice-making, even when it's bad. It's because if people have no free will, God could just push a button, and order, 'Worship Me!' and all mankind would bow down like robots. That's not the kind of relationship God wants with people."

You add, "And I really believe that God has even the bad things under control in some way."

- Second tough question: *Hasn't history shown that 'truth' is relative? What was true for people at one time, or place, or situation, might not be true for other people.*

There's an old joke: "Anyone who thinks truth is relative, doesn't know *my* relatives!"

A friend and I once talked with a University of Central Florida student in the collegiate housing area. His appearance: many facial piercings, spiked mohawk, and a really cool t-shirt with a bowl of crying vegetables saying, "Salads are Murder! He was gracious, intelligent, and said that although he was an atheist, his interest in spiritual issues was an 8 (on a scale of 1 to 10).

We had a good time talking with him for about 40 minutes, and he let us share the Gospel with him. I was impressed with how well he grasped the concepts of God's plan of salvation. He said he'd look up the Bible verses on-line, and "think about it."

Then I challenged him to read some of the New Testament and ask himself this question, "If this were true, what would the implications be?" He politely said he didn't think that was a very good question because "people are always trying to talk themselves into believing in things." I was amazed at this insight, and told him so. I asked him to still read the Bible passages, but forget the question.

As we left, I got thinking about our conversation. My asking this young man to evaluate the truthfulness of Scripture was a kind of old-fashioned philosophical challenge, dating back to a time when people assumed there *was* absolute truth and the goal was to find it. The modern thinking may be described as mild curiosity in other's beliefs, but with a clear understanding that those beliefs are relative to the people who believe them, and have no authority over anyone who doesn't.

The question of relativity regarding truth is rarely verbalized, but it is a *de facto* "given" among most non-Christian college students. Their environment on a university campus is one in which Christian professors are few, and accordingly, the idea that there is a source of eternal truth is most often dismissed. It's not an issue, I think, that occupies a lot of people's conscious thought, but it lurks under the surface of the modern day world culture.

Key concept: Truth that is considered "relative" is not actually truth. It would be more closely aligned to temporary measures designed to accommodate whatever the prevalent standard of behavior is for any given culture. The essential nature of this kind of "truth" is that it changes. The criteria for relative truth are not based upon ethics or morality, but upon whatever society—at least the most vocal parts of society—deems acceptable at the moment. In contrast, God's truth is unchanging and based upon consistent morality, ethics, and an accurate assessment of mankind's tendency to excuse sinful behavior.

Key verses:

Psalm 119:160 *The sum of Thy word is truth, and every one of Thy righteous ordinances is everlasting*

Matthew 24:35 *Heaven and earth will pass away, but My words shall not pass away.*

James 1:17. *. . . the Father . . . who does not change like shifting shadows.*

Here's our little dialogue:

Your friend asks "But isn't truth relative?"

You reply, "Well, I guess it depends on what you mean by relative . . ."

He or she says, "That truth changes. What was true a hundred years, or five hundred years ago, might not be true today. People thought the earth was flat. Now they know it isn't. Or, did you ever see the TV show, _____? There was one episode where they mocked an anti-gay woman by quoting the Bible about how many old Bible laws had changed. The point was that the anti-gay person was just out of touch."

"I heard about that one. But the pro-gay people were comparing symbolic, ceremonial Jewish law, like not weaving two kinds of fabric together, with moral law. Which is pretty lame. I mean, you wouldn't say that murder and dietary laws are in the same category. Does it make sense to you that ritual law and ethical or moral law are different?

Your friend shrugs. "Well whatever. Times change; rules change. What's the French expression, "other days, other ways."

"Okay, let me throw a tool of philosophy at you. One of the so-called tests in philosophy is to extend an idea to its logical extreme. Let's say we're talking about rules for life that are about morals, like stealing or killing. The question is, who decides what the rules are, and what do they base the rules on."

"Okay, keep going"

"If God exists and He's the one who makes the rules, then the rules would be permanent and wouldn't change. So we extend a rule like "don't murder" from Cain and Abel . . . yeah, I know, you think of them as myths, but bear with me . . . all the way to today. So God's law would say murder is just as wrong now as in ancient times."

Your friend replies, "Well, murder still *is* illegal, whether God makes the law or not."

"Not all killing is illegal. In some countries, euthanasia of the elderly or terminally ill is legal. And I know you don't like the issue of abortion, but even pro-choice people know it ends healthy life, so it is defined as killing. And on a big scale. There are eight states with smaller populations than the number of abortions in the US every year."

"Where is this going?"

"Just that relative truth is such a slippery slope. What people once hated . . . and were convinced was wrong . . . when it becomes legal, it becomes normal, and after a while most people don't even think about it. They just figure, 'That's the way it is.' So all I'm saying is that whether a person believes in God or not, when the right or wrong of life is left up to whatever is popular, or the 'intelligentsia,' or politicians looking for votes, it might be relative, but I don't call it truth anymore.

You add, "I guess my main point is that people really need absolute truth, and logically that can only come from God."

Your friend asks, "What do you mean, 'logically'?"

"Just that anything people come up with as true is going to be influenced by their own preferences, or the people in power, or what the masses feel at the moment. So it's logical that if it's going to be objective and long-lasting, it has to come from outside the human condition, meaning deity."

- Third tough question: *What about people who don't hear about Jesus Christ?*

  Key concept: The heart of this question, I think, is best summed up in this way: "Is God really loving, and is He fair?" If Jesus Christ is the only way to heaven, as He says, then what about all the people who never even hear about Jesus? How can we perceive God as loving, or just, when such a seemingly unfair situation exists? This is an important question because of the implications about the nature of

God: His fairness, and issues concerning the "availability" of His plan for salvation to all people.

We as Christians know from Scripture that there is no debate at all that acceptance of Jesus Christ as Savior is the only way any person is able to be saved and gain eternal life. *I am the way, and the truth, and the life; no one comes to the Father but through Me.* (John 14:6)

Salvation is found in no one else, there is no other name under heaven given to men by which we must be saved. (Acts 4: 12 NIV)

Why is there salvation in no one else, or any other religion? Because no other religion has a person *qualified* to pay the cost of people's sin. Only Jesus, God Himself, is acceptable as the payment. Other religions have only sinful humans who profess to lead the way to God, but they have nothing to atone for the wrongs people commit, merely rituals and practices that do not correct the sin nature. Salvation has nothing to do with good works or sincerity. The only relevant issue is sin. And the only effective cure for sin is God's forgiveness founded upon the sacrifice of the Lamb who is worthy.

In a very real sense, the world has one true religion, one obsolete religion (Judaism), and many false religions. Hebrews 8:13, referring to Judaism as the "first covenant," says . . . *He has made the first covenant obsolete. And whatever is becoming obsolete and growing old is ready to disappear.* This assessment may sound radically harsh, even to some modern Christians who may consider Judaism still a relevant path to God. But the purpose of Judaism was to establish the foundation for the coming Messiah, the Christ, and this has occurred. The Law of Moses did not make people sinless, or negate the consequences of sin, but rather made people aware of how much they needed a Messiah to do so.

Perhaps a better word than "obsolete" to describe Judaism—post Messiah— is "fulfilled." Judaism has fulfilled its purpose: to bring us Jesus, the Christ.

This truth, however, is not necessarily the best starting point with a non-Christian. Though true, it can seem intolerant or elitist to a unbeliever.

The important concept is that while we do not necessarily understand every detail of God's judgment of mankind, aborted babies, for example, we know that He is completely loving and just, and that we can trust His decisions in this matter.

Key verses: Lamentations 3:22,23 God is loving. *The steadfast love of the Lord never ceases. His mercies never come to an end; they are new every morning.* And 2 Peter 3:9 . . . *but (God) is patient toward you, not wishing for any to perish, but for all to come to repentance.* This is also why God, through Paul's writing, implores us to tell people about salvation through Christ. Romans 10:14 . . . *how will they believe in Him of whom they have not heard? And how will they hear without someone preaching to them?* 1 Corinthians 9:16 . . . *woe is me if I do not preach the gospel!*

Romans 3:5,6 God is just. *The God who (judges) is not unrighteous, is He? . . . May it never be! For otherwise how will God judge the world?*

While I hear this question mostly from younger adults, say the 20–25 age group, I've heard it from older folks as well. There are variations of this question, such as "What about babies?," or "What about those not able to understand the gospel?." People may ask this sincerely, with a genuine distress that God would be this way. Others may throw the question out simply to be aggravating to the believer who's trying to share with them. It's a legitimate question when sincerely posed. It's also a question that I, for one, don't have a definitive answer to. That is, how God resolves His perfect love and justice—in terms of the "technical" details—is beyond my comprehension. But let's take a look at a way we can respond to this tough question.

We'll assume that you've been able to share a gospel illustration with your friend. (See Question 4), and then she or he says,

"Yeah, what about those who never hear about Jesus? What's your God do with them?"

(By the way, remember, we don't preach at people. We talk with them. If you preach, many may tune you out. *'Come now, and let us reason together', says the Lord.* (Isaiah 1:18)

"Well," you say, "let's think of the alternatives. If there is no God, then none of this matters. Life is totally random. You live. You die. Whatever you do has no consequence. And the worms get a meal . . .

"How about option #2 – there is God, and everybody goes to heaven, the evil with the good. So any religion people have, or people with no religion . . . they still all go to heaven. That's called universalism, and it works if we don't care about justice."

"So. What's terrible about that?"

"Remember the man who kidnapped, tortured and killed the little girls? And smirked about it at his trial? Do you really think he could be in the presence of a holy God? Man, that'd be like a moth into a blast furnace."

"Okay," says your friend. "What if the good go to heaven and the bad ones don't? We'd even let God be the one who chooses."

"Aha! Good insight. You're seeing it from God's perspective, which is great. The problem with that is that while the good things we do *are* good—and God does appreciate them—they're just not good enough to make up for the selfish, bad stuff we do. It would be like saying that the healthy cells in our body will balance out the cancer cells. Just doesn't work that way. Plus, not to be crude, but the Bible says that the best deeds we do are like vomit-soaked rags compared to God's righteousness." (Isaiah 64:6)

"Okay, gross. But I get your analogy."

"Of course, that man that killed the children, if he genuinely hated what he did, and asked Christ to forgive him, then he would be okay. But not because what he did wasn't terrible."

Your friend says, "Yeah, I get that, but it still seems harsh."

"Well, that's why that one statement we talked about—that Jesus died for us while we are still doing wrong, selfish stuff—is key. What was really harsh is the one person who didn't deserve to be hurt, Jesus, was . . . for a reason, to pay for the bad things we do. God would be foolish if there was an easier way to rescue humans. Jesus dying in our place is the *least* God could do to solve the problem . . .and it was the *most* He could do."

"Okay, I see that. But again, bottom line, what about all the people who never hear about Jesus? "

(You've presented what you know to be true. Now you can, if you're like me in this regard, say what is also true: that there're exact parts of this you don't understand. It's not only okay to admit to people when you don't understand something, it's good to do so.)

"I'll tell you straight up that I *do not* understand all about this," you say. "And I agree with you that it's a huge question. I guess what I can say is that I know for sure that He's far more loving, and far more fair than I am. So I totally trust Him to resolve this in His way, whether I see how He does it or not.

"There's a couple of statements that back up that position. One just says that God does care about people, and He's wants to show us that every day. (Lamentations 3:22,23) The other statement sounds a bit harsh, but it's good. It says that our sense of what's fair is way more prejudiced and weaker than God's, and that's why He is the best person to judge people (Romans 3:5,6). There's also one statement that I think is really serious. It says that the destiny of every person is death, and then they face God's judgment (Hebrews 9:27). I believe that, and that's why I tell people about Christ."

Question 6

What are evidences for the existence of God?

IN 2014, IN AN interview with Pablo Jaurequi, of *El Mundo*, * physicist Steven Hawking stated categorically that God does not exist, adding "I am an atheist." He said that "Before we understand science, it is natural to believe that God created the universe. But now science offers a more convincing explanation." Hawking was considered by some to be one of the smartest persons alive, but the Bible presents a different explanation for Stephen Hawking's dismissal of God. (* Hawking, *El Mundo*, September 23, 2014)

> *The fool has said in his heart, "There is no God"* (Psalm 53:1)

> *Professing to be wise, they became fools . . . for they exchanged the truth of God for a lie . . .* (Romans 1: 22,25)

It is helpful in ministry, however, to think in terms of how people in contemporary American culture might view the issue of God's existence. This is especially relevant, I think, on college campuses, as the environment on universities can be generally described as secular and non-theistic. Most students we talk with about matters of faith are too polite to come right out and declare that they don't believe in God, but, as one student put it, " I tell my parents I believe in God, but I really don't. The idea of God seems pretty irrelevant to my life."

It's a type of functional atheism. There seems to be little interest on campus today to espouse a militant atheistic stance, vehemently arguing against God's existence. Instead, the overall feeling we get from university students is polite indifference about the subject.

Given that atmosphere, how can we introduce the concept of God's existence in a manner that doesn't sound "religious" to modern people, but still opens up the subject in a way that gives us some leverage to present the gospel?

Our great assurance when we share God's word is that the Word itself and the Holy Spirit cause it to be effective. The challenge in our secular culture today is to find a way to share.

So this little discussion about the existence of God is meant to be an conversational aid to bridge the secular / Christian gap to help us get into the position where we can share the gospel.

Here are what I think are five sort-of-logical, semi-empirical "evidences" for the existence of God:

The 5 evidences spelled out

1. One "evidence" is a person's recognition and appreciation of the ordered complexity and beauty of the natural world. Mutation is never orderly or beautiful. *For since the creation of the world, His invisible attributes, His eternal power and divine nature have been clearly seen, being understood through what has been made . . .* (Romans 1: 20) Growing up as a kid in a tiny New England town, I'd often climb the hill behind our house during Christmas break, and look down over the snow-covered town. It was a classic post-card setting, and in the evenings all one could see were trees and Christmas lights on scattered houses. There was a Congregational church in the town below, and it rang its bells every hour. It was dark, cold, and usually snowing, but I remember feeling a sense of awe, and wondering if there really was a God.

2. A correct and positive sense of self-worth.. . . *for I am fearfully and wonderfully made . . . and my soul knows it very well.* (Psalm 139:14) I find it interesting that this Scripture says it is "my soul" that "knows it very well" that he or she is fearfully (or carefully) and wonderfully made. Our mind might not acknowledge this wonderfulness. Our insecurities might rather cause us to compare ourselves with others and

be dissatisfied. But deep down, our soul knows very well that we really are uniquely wonderful. In ministry, we have observed that though some people may wish they had better gifts or abilities in comparison with others, they do not wish they were actually a different person. I believe this is a profound sense of self-value that comes from God, and speaks to His nature and existence.

3. An intrinsic knowledge of what is true and right, versus what is false and wrong ... i.e. conscience.. ... *when those who do not have the Law do instinctively the things of the Law . . . they show the work of the Law written in their hearts, their conscience bearing witness, and their thoughts alternately accusing or else defending them.* (Romans 2:14,15) It's good to note this Bible passage states that it is not only believers in God who have consciences which convict them of right and wrong, but non-believers as well. Their consciences "bear witness" in such a way that the people's thoughts either defend their actions as right, or accuse them of having done wrong. And though verse 14 refers to the Mosaic Law, I feel the context of this passage in the letter Paul wrote to the church in Rome alludes to ethical and moral convictions of the Law (e.g. honesty, sexual decency), rather than the ceremonial or symbolic aspects. In other words, I don't believe a non-religious person would by accused by his or her conscience of wrongdoing for eating an eel, but be at peace about having trout for lunch (Deuteronomy 14:9,10 dietary laws). Their conscience would, however, accuse or defend them in matters of honesty, integrity, or morality. Of course, peoples' consciences can be ignored or deadened. .. *through the hypocrisy of liars, seared in their own conscience as with a branding iron* ... (1 Timothy 4:1,2) as distinct from:. . . . *do my best to maintain always a blameless conscience both before God and before men.* (Acts 24:16) Never-the-less, almost without exception, college students we talk with readily admit to having pretty clear moral codes they try to live by, and that they are well aware of when, and to what degree, they fail in keeping their own code.

4. Our giftedness.. ... *what do you have that you did not receive? But if you did receive it, why do you boast as if you had not received it?* (1 Corinthians 4:7) The idea here is that even non-believers are aware of—and appreciative of—their own talents and gifts. Once, a friend and I were talking with two young men in apartment near a campus. Their basic attitude about God and faith was one of amused indifference. One of

them turned out to be a line-backer for the college team; the other played guitar in an amateur band. The musician even admitted to us that he was "pretty good." So we presented to them the idea that their own giftedness pointed to the existence of God. My friend cited the above statement (1 Corinthians 4:7) and basically said, "You guys are definitely gifted, and your abilities came from somewhere. You didn't create your natural skills by yourselves." The interesting thing about this interaction with these guys was that they both felt flattered that we were acknowledging their gifting, but a little startled because we had brought up something they had never considered. A natural athlete or gifted musician knows that he or she did not create that talent for themselves. It was given to them . . . by someone. The evidence for God here is that He is the giver of those gifts.

5. The "witness" of an obedient Christian's life. *Let your light shine before men in such a way that they may see your good works, and glorify your Father who is in heaven.* (Matthew 5:16) A campus minister and I were meeting with a student (philosophy major) who had asked us to help him investigate the Christian faith. His starting point was an interesting one: he wasn't at all sure God even existed, but he was very impressed with the Christian students he knew. That was his motive for searching for the truth about God. A genuine Christian life, manifest in a normal, everyday human being *is* impressive . . . not dramatically impressive perhaps to a generation used to instant special effects . . . but impressive in a cumulative way. That's what this philosophy major saw in his Christian friends, some of whom he had known for years. What seemed to him both puzzling and encouraging was the undeniable reality of Christ-likeness in those friends. One of my friends once said, "Jesus is the *person-version* of God." I like that. Scripture clearly states that we can look at Jesus and discover the nature, glory, and character of God the Father, because Jesus "explains" God to us!

> *And the Word became flesh and dwelt among us, and we beheld His glory, glory as of the only begotten of the Father . . . No man has seen God at any time; the only begotten, who is in the bosom of the Father, He has explained Him.* (John 1:14, 18)

> *Philip said to Him 'Lord, show us the Father, and it will be enough for us.' Jesus said . . . 'He who has seen Me has seen the Father . . .'* (John 14: 8,9)

And He (Jesus) is the radiance of His glory and the exact representation of His nature . . . (Hebrews 1: 3)

A serious Christian bears this same likeness. *But we all, with unveiled faces beholding as in a miror the glory of the Lord, are being transformed into the same image from glory to glory . . . (2 Corinthians 3:18)*

This evidence is a subtle one. Not all non-believers are aware of the qualities of life in others. But for those who are, this is a powerful lever of credibility for the love of God and His power to change lives.

Let me bring up one last consideration. This is not really an "evidence" of God's existence, but a tool I believe presents Christianity as the only convincing "philosophy of life". It's a five-question *test* for whether a philosophy is true or valid.

Here are the five questions (or criteria):

1. Is the essential principle of the philosophy logical, and can be understood with the mind, not mystical or transcendental?

2. Does the philosophy apply to all people, not just the intellectual, gifted, privileged, etc.?

3. Does the philosophy address the reality of life as most people acknowledge it? That is, does it recognize the inherent sinfulness of man, but also his ability to do good. In other words, whatever the philosophy is, that it is not unrealistically grim (nihilism) or unrealistically optimistic (utopian image of "how man could be").

4. Does the philosophy attempt to answer the deep questions of the ages, e.g. "What is the purpose of life?" "What happens after death?" "What is truth?"

5. Does the philosophy provide actual guidance for how a person can achieve the goal of the philosophy?

Examples of applying these criteria to certain concepts might be as follows:

Socialism – Violates test #3, that it addresses the reality of life and people, in that it presumes that if people are adequately provided for, selfish greed and hostility would cease.

Existentialism – Ignores test # 4, as existentialism sees all existence as "absurd," that is, meaningless, and therefore such issues as purpose and truth are irrelevant.

Mysticism – fails test #1, since mysticism is by definition, *ineffable*, that is, mystical experience cannot be understood outside the experience itself.

Christianity – Meets these criteria for validity.

It is reasonable – *'Come now, and let us reason together,' says the Lord.* (Isaiah 1:18) *So he* (Paul) *was reasoning in the synagogue with the Jews and the God-fearing Gentiles . . .* (Acts 17:17)

It applies to all people –*. . . not wishing for any to perish but for all to come to repentance . . . whoever will call upon the name of the Lord will be saved.* (2 Peter 3:9 & Romans 10:13)

It accurately addresses the reality of people's nature –*. . . there is no difference, for all have sinned and fall short of the glory of God.* (Romans 3:22,23) But Luke 7:1ff describes a centurion who was called good, "worthy," and one who loves God.

It answers the deep questions of life. Purpose: *God . . . gave us the ministry of reconciliation . . . Therefore, we are ambassadors for Christ, as though God were entreating through us.* (2 Corinthians 5:18,20) Life after death: *When Christ, who is our life, is revealed, then you also will be revealed with Him in glory.* (Colossians 3:4)

It gives clear directions for being a success as a Christian –*. . . Scripture is inspired by God and profitable for teaching, for reproof, for correction, for training in righteousness; that the person of God may be adequate, equipped for every good work.* (2 Timothy 3:16,17)

Conclusion: "Seek and you will find" applies here. I believe if a person is sincerely trying to discover if God exists, then God will allow Himself to be found by that person. None of these is probably compelling evidences to a hard-core skeptic, but we're really just looking to plant seeds for non-theists to consider, to gain enough credibility so that we might share the Gospel with them.

Question 7:

How can I feel confident that I'm interpreting the Bible correctly?

Logic and hermeneutics

FIRST, LET'S BRIEFLY DISCUSS how simple logic works in language to determine what's understandable and accurate in Bible interpretation. I believe an understanding of logic is a much ignored, but helpful tool in accurate Bible interpretation.

Basic Aristotelian logic:

The purpose of logic (logical reasoning) is to provide a way to discuss issues so that the conclusion arrived at is consistent with the terms and values used in the discussion. Please note – even if the presentation of an issue is logical, it is not necessarily true. And conversely, if an argument is illogical, that does not necessarily mean that it is untrue. A truth may be presented in an illogical manner.

The basic form of classical logic is the syllogism. A syllogism is a set of statements (premises) leading to a logical, inevitable conclusion.

Example:

Premise # 1 Shane got an "A" on an algebra test.

Premise #2 Heather got a "B" on an algebra test.

Premise # 3 Jacob got a "C" on an algebra test.

Conclusion: Therefore, Shane achieved a higher grade on the algebra test than Jacob or Heather.

This is logical because the "value" of the grading system is understandable and accepted; that is, the closer the letter grade to the beginning of the alphabet, the higher the grade: A = highest, B= next highest, etc.

But an illogical conclusion of this same example would be that "Shane is smarter than Jacob or Heather." Why? Because the "value" being tested is not intelligence but simply who got the higher grade on a particular algebra test. Heather may be more intelligent than Shane, but had a bad testing day, or just doesn't do well in math, or any number of reasons she scored lower than Shane on this particular algebra test.

Could this illogical conclusion be true? Yes, it *could be* true that Shane is more intelligent than Jacob or Heather—though that is a far more complex determination—but that was not what the syllogism was about.

The most common logical fallacies are these:

- "non sequitur " (means "it does not follow") When the key term or value used in the premises of the argument is vague, or changes meaning from one premise to the other premises.Example: As in the little syllogism above, about the algebra test, when the "value" that was at the heart of the syllogism—who got the highest score on the test—was changed to who was the most intelligent . . . the key value was so changed as to make the comparison illogical. This change of values can be quite obvious, as in this silly example:

    premise 1: good books make good friends

    premise 2: a dog is a man's best friend

    conclusion: therefore, a dog is a good book.

    Obviously, the value of "friend" changed radically, making the syllogism ridiculous.

    In a Christian context, the non-sequitur argument has been used to justify a type of "soft" universalism. This argument was based simply on the verses that say Jesus died for "all." The argument for universal salvation states that the Bible "says 'all' and it means 'all.'" Yet the grammar of those verses clearly indicates that the meaning is that "all' refers to those person who are eligible for salvation, not that every person is automatically saved. This demonstrates an obvious *shift* in meaning of the two uses of "all," yet some people I have talked to about this issue did not discern the change in meaning. This is disappointing, as the change is not subtle.

I wish I could say I believe most Christians have an accurate sense of discernment in noticing when Bible teachers change the meaning of a key word, for instance, in a sermon or lecture. I think it happens quite often, however, without being noticed.

- "ad hominem" (means "to the man" or "against the man") When one arguer in a discussion attacks the character or integrity of his opponent rather than the opponent's stance on the issue. We certainly see these personal attacks often wielded in politics.

  Example: "How can you take the word of this man who cheated on his wife!" (This could also be a non-sequitur if the term "cheated" refers to cheating at cards rather than marital infidelity).

  In biblical context, the teaching of a particular Christian leader may be dismissed because of the personal failings of that person. While it is certainly true that often a false teacher's life does not stand up well to scrutiny, it does not mean that any person with a sin issue is a false teacher. A pastor (e.g.) may fall into some type of sinful behavior, yet have taught, and continues to teach, solid biblical truth.

- "false dilemma" The word "dilemma" means a situation in which a decision must be made in which there are only two choices, and that the two choices are usually the extremes of each other.

  - Example from the 1950's: "If America does not stop the spread of Communism in Korea, the whole world will eventually become Communististic."

  - Biblical context example: "If you're not a Calvinist, you're an Armenian." In such a case, a person holding a particular theological viewpoint tries to strengthen his or her position by placing people with other theological views in an opposite extreme. The problem with a forced dilemma is that it dismisses reasonable (and biblical) alternatives to the two extremes, such as a person whose position is that while recognizing God's sovereignty and intervention in human life, also believes that people have a freedom to make choices.

- "false analogy" An "analogy" is a comparison between two situations intended to clarify an issue by presenting a simplistic picture of a complex condition.
  - Example: In the 2014 movie, *The Imitation Game*,* about the life and work of Alan Turing, especially relating to the Enigma project of WWII, the films screenwriter, Graham Moore, was criticized for historical inaccuracy in "suggesting that Turing was the only cryptographer working on it, with others either not helping or outright opposed . . . when in fact, it was a collaborative, not individual effort." (* Wikipedia article on *The Imitation Game*.) "In a 2015 interview * with The Huffington Post, Graham Moore said in response to complaints about the film's historical accuracy: '. . . .I think this fundamentally misunderstands how art works. You don't fact check Monet's *Water Lilies*. That's not what water lilies look like. . . .'" (* Katz, Writer Slams 'Fact-Checking Films, January 8, 2015) The reason this is a false analogy is that the comparison between an artist's conception of water lilies, and which humans actually contributed to an important historical event (cracking the German code in WWII) compares unlike situations. To deprive the real collaborators on the Enigma project of their contribution to ending a world war is essentially different from an artist portraying a pond lily in a stylized manner.
  - Biblical example: I once heard a speaker make a comparison between the proselytizing activities of the scribes and Pharisees, and Christians who go door-to-door in campus dorms trying to share the gospel of Christ. *'Woe to you, scribes and Pharisees, hypocrites, because you travel about on sea and land to make one proselyte, and when he becomes one, you make him twice as much a son of hell as yourselves.'* (Matthew 23:15) The speaker's point in this comparison was that he felt that the bold evangelism he cited was both unnecessary and offensive. He then quoted the apocryphal saying, "Preach the gospel at all times. If necessary, use words." (attributed to Francis of Assisi) The speaker's meaning was that the evidence of your life is all that's really needed, and that actually speaking the gospel is a secondary, less effective, option.

- Biblically, using words to preach the gospel is indeed necessary. *How then shall they call upon Him in whom they have not believed? And how shall they believe in Him whom they have not heard? And how shall they hear without a preacher?* (Romans 10:14)

- The speaker's analogy, or comparison, was flawed because he equated bold evangelism, which is commanded (2 Timothy 4:2,5) and praised: *. . . how beautiful are the feet of those who bring glad tidings . . .* (Romans 10:15)—with the Pharisees striving to get others to join them in religious hypocrisy.

- The "fallacy of tautology." (Literally, "needless repetition of meaning" or something that is supposedly "self-evidently" true.) This simply means that something is not necessarily true just because it is frequently and/or forcefully stated to be true. A person may feel that a position he holds is obviously true, that it is self-evident that it is true, and he may state this often and passionately as a self-evident truth. But this does not make it true, logically.

  - A common example is when someone states an opinion as an indisputable fact. We may see this logical error in cultural issues, e.g. the theory of Darwinian evolution. A biology textbook titled *Life On Earth* * introduces its chapter, "The Process of Evolution," this way: "Evolution – is it a fact or a theory? This question echoes an old and virulent controversy. It is important not only historically but because of the light it can shed on the distinction scientists make between fact and theory. The process of evolution is a fact. It occurs." (* *Life On Earth*, p. 769) Obviously, the editors of this college textbook feel very strongly that Darwinian evolution is true, which is their privilege. But to state that it is true in such an irrefutable manner, in spite of the numerous objections to it, including by secular scientists, puts this statement into the category of a fallacy of tautology.

  - Biblical context example: This happens a lot, I think, often in well-intentioned ways. That is, someone may endorse a particular approach to some aspect of ministry that depends upon a premise; let's say the premise is that "most people are not aware of their own sinfulness." This may or may not be true, but the approach to this particular, hypothetical, ministry style would focus on ways to point out people's sinfulness and its consequences. Again, this may or may not be true, but simply stating that it is true, irrefutably true, is an indicator that the fallacy of tautology might be being used to bolster the ministry's emphasis.

- Ironically, one of the indicators of the logical fallacy of tautology is if a position is proclaimed to be "truth." A classic example of this is the documentary titled "An Inconvenient Truth," * concerning the subject of global warming. The title assumes that the position of the documentary is obviously true, and that those who oppose this position do so because it inconveniences them. Again, remember, we're not trying to determine the validity of issues, simply the logic of the arguments about the issues. (* Guggenheim, Davis, and Gore, Al, *An Inconvenient Truth*, 2006)

Whew! Sorry for the lengthy spiel on logic, but I think it's important to be sure we're thinking objectively before we discuss hermeneutics, the guidelines for good Bible interpretation.

Hermeneutics: Guidelines for Bible interpretation

Basic suppositions:

- That the Bible is God's true Word to mankind. . . . *seeing that His divine power has granted to us everything pertaining to life and godliness through the true knowledge of Him . . . But know this first of all, that no prophecy of Scripture is a matter of one's own interpretation, for no prophecy was ever made by an act of human will, but men moved by the Holy Spirit spoke from God.* (2 Peter 1:3 & 20, 21)

- That God's Word is useful for Christians to be mature and serve God. *All Scripture is inspired by God and profitable for teaching, for reproof, for correction, for training in righteousness; that the man of God may be adequate, equipped for every good work.* (2 Timothy 3:16,17)

- That it is our responsibility to accurately interpret Scripture, not a pastor's or a commentary writer's. While these are good resources, we, like the Bereans, should. . . *examining the Scriptures daily, to see whether these things were so.* (Acts 17:11)

Basic requirements:

- Be a believer — *But a natural man does not accept the things of the Spirit of God; for they are foolishness to him, and he cannot understand them, because they are spiritually appraised.* (1 Corinthians 2:12–16)
- Want to know what it means so you can do it — *If any man is willing to do His will, he shall know of the teaching, whether it is of God . . .* (John 7:17)
- Set aside your own preferences, "pre-judicial" opinions, your doctrinal "up bringing," and experiences. Don't seek to make Scripture rubber-stamp or validate your own particular preferences. This doesn't mean that we have to discard valuable experiences or a solid Christian upbringing. It means that when we interpret Scripture, we do so with as little personal bias as possible.
- Commit to apply Scripture when you understand it. The Bible is meant to change our lives, not just increase our knowledge. *But prove yourselves doers of the Word, and not merely hearers, who delude themselves.* (James 1:22)
- Be willing to live with Biblical ambiguity. Don't be tempted to tie up "loose ends" just to have a difficult issue settled. . . . *learn not to exceed what is written . . .* (1 Corinthians 4:6).

Basic guidelines:

- *Consider the language.* Understand that language in the Bible, and language in general, states things explicitly, implicitly, or by inference.
    a. explicitly – that is, it says it in clear, easy-to-understand terms e.g *Flee immorality.* (1 Corinthians 6:18) No confusion here . . . don't sin sexually.
    b. implicitly – that is, it *implies* a truth or command. *You shall not covet your neighbor's . . . ox or his donkey . . .* (Exodus 20:17) So before I think to myself, "All right! I'm off the hook; my neighbor doesn't even have an ox or donkey!" I easily realize that the verse also implies that I shouldn't covet my neighbor's Lexus or swimming pool. The meaning of the command is

clear. The objects of the coveting just need to be updated. This is implication.

c. by inference – Inference is a bit more removed from the clear and easy applications of explicit or implicit meanings. Inference can require some logical thought. I like to think of inference as two boards joined by overlapping them a good amount before they are nailed or glued together. Can you picture that? The joint will be strong and the second board will be lined up with the first one. Now picture two boards which someone is trying to join butt-end to butt-end. It's almost impossible to join boards this way; the joint would be weak at best, and the second board might not be aligned with the first.

The point? Inference considers a principle of Scripture and re-applies it to a different situation, but with the new situation accurately lined up with the principle. The two boards touching end-to-end, as an example of Bible application, would be conjectural. A conjecture is a guess. Even if it's an educated or interesting guess, it's still a guess.

God's parting and drying up of the Red Sea (Exodus 14:21), can be inferred as a principle that God will provide a way of escape to His people. The inference of the principle can be seen in 1 Corinthians 10:13 concerning God's provision of escape in times of temptation. *. . . but with the temptation will provide the way of escape also, that you may be able to endure it.* So even though the Red Sea event and an escape from a modern-day temptation are quite different, the inference is valid and biblical.

An example of *conjecture* might be illustrated by a sermon I once heard entitled "They dropped the ropes." It looked at the passage in Mark chapter 2 in which a paralytic is lowered down through the roof of a house where Jesus is, that the man might be healed. The sermon conjectured that the friends of the paralytic had so much faith that their friend would be healed—and that they would not have to haul him back up—they dropped the ropes by which they lowered him. It was an intriguing interpretation of that event, but there was no Scriptural basis to say it actually happened. While conjecture can be fascinating, deriving an application or principle from it can be misleading.

- *Try to get the exact meaning of key words*, e.g. "baptism"

- *Consider the grammar of the passage.* I know, groan! This is not always an easy task. For example, look at the introduction to Paul's letter to Titus.

  Paul, a bond servant of God, and an apostle of Jesus Christ, for the faith of those chosen of God and the knowledge of the truth which is according to godliness, in the hope of eternal life, which God, who cannot lie, promised ages ago, but at the proper time manifested, even His word, in the proclamation with which I was entrusted according to the commandment of God our Savior; to Titus, my true child... (Titus 1:1–4)

  Wow, try to unravel the grammar of that sentence! Yes, it was one sentence. The basic communication is, "Paul... to Titus," with a whole lot of qualifiers and additional information thrown in. The point is that it's pretty easy to get overwhelmed by all the information in long, complicated passages. Having a grasp—at least in a basic way— of the sentence structure helps us keep the writer's intent clear.

- *Consider the type of literature*... history, poetry, doctrine etc. This is very important so we don't try, for example, to build a doctrinal position on a passage of Scripture that isn't intended to be doctrinal. As an illustration, some of the imprecatory Psalms ("imprecatory" meaning "to invoke a curse against") are obviously the psalmist "venting" his anger and wrath against God's enemies. E.g. *How blessed will be the one who seizes and dashes your little ones against the rocks.* (Psalm 137:9) This is definitely not a verse upon which to base a doctrine for ministry!

  Is it "literal" or figurative? How do we distinguish which is which? Sometimes it is obvious whether the language is meant to be figurative or literal. But there are other cases in which more careful evaluation is necessary.

  How about this image in Psalm 78:65 *Then the Lord awoke as if from sleep, like a warrior overcome by wine.* In the margin of my Bible from years ago, I have written, "What??!!" Obviously, this is figurative.

  Also think about Jesus' statement in Luke 14:26 *'If anyone comes to Me, and does not hate his own father and mother and wife and children and brothers and sisters, yes, and even his own life, he cannot be My disciple.'* We must take into account that Jesus is using hyperbole, a deliberately forceful phrasing to emphasize that following Him as His disciple means to make Him pre-eminent of all other relationships. Otherwise we might conclude Jesus is espousing hatred.

Or, for example, the terrible creatures described in Revelation 9:7–10 their appearance was *like horses . . . like the faces of men . . . hair like the hair of women . . . teeth like the teeth of lions . . .* etc. So the use of simile—in this case, the word, "like—or the use of metaphor helps us to see when something is symbolic or figurative.

Conversely, Revelation 20:10 & 15 states,

> *And the devil who deceived them was thrown into the lake of fire and brimstone, where the beast and the false prophet are also, and they will be tormented day and night forever and ever. . . . And if anyone's name was not written in the book of life, he was thrown into the lake of fire.*

There is no use of simile here. The lake of fire and the eternal torment of Satan, the false prophet, the beast, and unbelievers are presented as literal, not figurative.

- *Consider to whom it is written.* It can make a difference in our understanding of a passage to know who the intended readership is. In Paul's letter to the church at Rome, which he had, apparently, never visited, he stresses the doctrine of salvation based upon faith alone (Romans 4:1–5) This makes perfect sense. Paul would lay out the essential foundations of the faith to this large church in the very heart of the Roman empire.

  In contrast, James' letter to the Christians "dispersed abroad" (James 1:1) emphasizes the necessary obedience of everyday Christian life, including good works. *What use is it, my brethren, if a man says he has faith, but has no works? Can that faith save him?* (James 2:14) This statement might generate confusion if we considered it in isolation, that is, ignoring James' exhortation to Christians to affirm their salvation by faith as evidenced by their good works. James is basically saying, "Since you're saved, demonstrate that salvation by doing good works."

- *Consider the context.* As with the above consideration of intended audience, this doesn't always affect the interpretation of the Bible passage, but sometimes it helps to have a basic understanding of what was going on at the time, and what the society was like. But a word of caution here: we don't need to be exhaustive scholars of ancient history, or sociologists, to understand the Bible. The inspired Scriptures ("living and active"), with guidance by the Holy Spirit, can be understood by well-intentioned readers seeking for truth. The context is helpful in a secondary sense, but should not be the primary tool to grasp the Bible's meaning.

Here are two examples of cultural context, concerning the city of Corinth and the letters of Paul to the church at Corinth. This was a wild and immoral city, noted for every type of bad behavior. Paul's preaching on issues of moral laxity . . . *immorality of such a kind as does not even exist among the Gentiles* . . . (1 Corinthians 5:1) was directed to the people of this church as a very relevant topic. He also gave the Corinthian believers this advice about marriage: *But if they do not have self-control, let them marry; for it is better to marry than burn.* (1 Corinthians 7:9) The context—of the lustful depiction of the culture of Corinth—lets us correctly interpret this verse as "burn with passion or lust," rather than burn in the lake of fire.

- *Take into consideration all relevant passages* and verses in Scripture. Take the time to use a concordance or cross-reference tool to find as many passages as possible that relate to the issue. *The sum of thy word is truth* . . . (Psalm 119:160)

- *Do not allow a vague passage or verse to cast doubt upon a clear verse or passage.* That is, don't interpret a clear statement (e.g. about salvation) by reference to an unclear statement. Don't doubt an easily understood verse or passage because of a vague verse on the same subject. To do so may give rise to the so-called "contradictions" opponents of the Bible love to cite. As in this case:

    . . . who came down and prayed for them, that they might receive the Holy Spirit, for He had not yet fallen upon them; they had simply been baptized in the name of the Lord Jesus. Then they began laying hands on them, and they were receiving the Holy Spirit. (Acts 8: 15–17)

    These three verses—and only these three verses— seem to imply that people can be saved Christians, yet not have the Holy Spirit indwelling them. This brief passage has perhaps been the basis of an entire theology of "second blessing" experiences, in which believers in Christ are informed that being a Christian doesn't necessarily mean that they have the Holy Spirit. Though logic seems to suggest that it is absurd to possess 2/3 of the "triune" God, yet this position has numerous adherents.

While this passage is certainly puzzling, and many opinions have been offered as to its meaning, there are other Scriptures which maintain that all true believers in Christ have the Holy Spirit living in them.

... if anyone does not have the Spirit of Christ, he does not belong to Him. (Romans 8:9b)

In Him, you also, after listening to the message of truth, the gospel of your salvation—having also believed, you were sealed in Him with the Holy Spirit ... (Ephesians 1:13,14)

But the one who joins himself with the Lord is one spirit with Him ... do you not know that your body is a temple of the Holy Spirit who is in you, whom you have from God ... (1 Corinthians 6:17 & 19)

We surely don't ever throw away any verse of Scripture, but there are some in which the exact meaning may be elusive, and these we assess carefully taking into account other relevant verses and passages in which the meaning is clear.

- *When two conflicting doctrines seem to be both well supported biblically, they should both be accepted as Scriptural*, with the assurance that the conflict is resolved in God's mind.

  "pre-determinism"? *... for though the twins were not yet born, and had not yet done anything good or bad, in order that God's purpose according to His choice might stand ... said to her* (Rebekah) *'The older will serve the younger.'* (Romans 9: 11,12)

  "free will"? – *For there is no distinction ... for the Lord is the Lord of all, abounding in riches for all who call upon Him; for 'Whoever will call upon the Lord will be saved.'* (Romans 10: 12,13)

  In some matters of Bible interpretation, we will simply have to accept that we don't understand it completely, and probably won't. God Himself alludes to this, through Isaiah, in Isaiah 55:9 *For as the heavens are higher than the earth, so are My ways higher than your ways, and My thoughts than your thoughts.*

Be willing to live with loose ends.

Conclusion: Charles Ryrie's comment in the introduction to his study Bible * is this: "In the plain meaning of the text there is ample material for the Holy Spirit to speak to you and meet your individual needs." In other words, the common sense meaning of a Bible passage is most often the correct one. (* Ryrie, *The Ryrie Study Bible*, p. vii)

Question 8

What is worship?

WORSHIP IS A WORD we often hear these days in our Christian community. Pastors might ask one another, amusingly, "How many do you *worship* on Sunday morning?" meaning, of course, how many attend the Sunday services.

Most church-goers would refer to the gathering of the church as the "worship service," and perhaps think of the music, especially emotionally-intense music, as the essence of worship. In some churches, the person on stage leading the music is called the "worship leader." And in many contemporary church services, this is not someone leading the *congregation* in singing, but the leader of the group of musicians and singers on the stage, with little participation by the people attending church. Indeed, some of the "worship times" seem more like a concert than a congregation raising their voices in song.

What then *is* worship?

The word comes from the Anglo-Saxon and French words for "worth" and "ship." The meaning is to show reverence, adoration, honor, and veneration for a being *worthy* of such attention. Improper worship would be to show this attention to someone or an object which is not worthy, i.e. idolatry.

The essential concept of worship, then, is to acknowledge God as the only being who is worthy of such adoration, reverence, and honor.

The clearest familiar Scriptural example, I believe, is found in Revelation

> . . . *the twenty-four elders will fall down before Him who sits on the throne, and will worship Him who lives forever and ever, and will*

> *cast their crowns before the throne, saying, 'Worthy art Thou, our Lord and our God, to receive glory and honor and power; for Thou didst create all things, and because of Thy will they existed, and were created.'* (4:10,11)

Here is the essence of worship: the living, eternal God who is worthy, and the recognition of God's worthiness expressed in praise and falling down before the throne of God.

That's the scene in heaven. What does worship look like on earth today? Here are a few verses of Scripture that give insight into the nature of worship:

This passage describes a dialog between Jesus and the "woman at the well." (The woman says,) . . .

> *'Our fathers worshiped in this mountain, and you people* (i.e. Jews) *say that in Jerusalem is the place where men ought to worship.' Jesus said to her, 'Woman, believe Me, an hour is coming when neither in this mountain, nor in Jerusalem, shall you worship the Father . . . (23) But an hour is coming, and now is, when the true worshipers shall worship the Father in spirit and in truth; for such people the father seeks to be His worshipers. God is spirit, and those who worship Him must worship in spirit and truth.'* (John 4: 20–24)

Two key points about worship are made clear in this passage. First, that the location, or place, is irrelevant regarding true worship. Neither the mountain near Sychar, Samaria, nor the city of Jerusalem, is the place to worship God, Jesus tells the woman. Hence, a church building—or whatever location that a local church meets— is not any more a place of worship than a person's kitchen or garage, if that is where a person is worshiping in "sprit and in truth."

Jesus said the Father seeks true worshipers who will worship Him in spirit and in truth. What does this mean? I believe "in spirit" means, not some mystical state of being, but simply a true sincerity of heart, acknowledging the worthiness of God to receive one's praise and reverence. Contrast this to passages in Scripture which portray shallow, or going-through-the-motions worship. *This people honors Me with their lips, but their heart is far away from Me . . . in vain do they worship Me.* (Matthew 15:8,9). *Bring your worthless offerings no longer . . . I cannot endure iniquity and the solemn assembly.* (Isaiah 1: 13) Here we see the pretense of a "solemn assembly" by these false worshipers, bringing to God what He calls "worthless offerings."

This is the stuff of gross hypocrisy, pretending to worship God, but making a sham of the heart of true worship.

What is the "truth" which Jesus told the woman was essential for worship? Paul speaks to the men of Athens about the true *object* of worship.

> *Men of Athens, I observe that you are very religious in all respects, for while I was passing through and examining the objects of your worship, I also found an altar with this inscription, 'TO AN UNKNOWN GOD.' What therefore you worship in ignorance, this I proclaim to you. The God who made the world and all the things in it, since He is Lord of heaven and earth, does not dwell in temples made with hands; neither is He served by human hands, as though He needed anything, since He Himself gives to all life and breath . . .* (Acts 17:22, 23)

This passage is a wonderful example of Paul's boldness yet sensitivity. He praises the men of Athens for being "very religious in all respects," then he goes on to inform them that *what* they are worshiping is not worthy of that worship. In fact, they had so many objects of worship, that they even built an "unknown" one just to make sure all their religious bets were covered.

Paul explains to them that the true God is the Creator who gives life and breath to them—rather than they who create and maintain the idols of their worship. The point here is that even if people's worship is sincere, it must be accorded to the true God, not an unworthy idol. To worship an unworthy idol is, in Paul's words, ignorant, even if well intentioned. Paul even says this of the Jewish people who do not understand about Jesus, the Messiah. *I bear them witness that they have a zeal for God, but not in accordance with knowledge.* (Romans 10:2)

Here's another aspect of worship:

> *I urge you therefore, brethren, by the mercies of God, to present your bodies a living and holy sacrifice, acceptable to God, which is your spiritual service of worship.* (Romans 12:1)]

This verse condenses some great principles of our "spiritual service of worship." This is a "worship service" for us as individual Christians. Here's my paraphrase: Paul says, "I urge you to recognize God's mercy in forgiving and saving you. Because of this, even your physical bodies are now holy, so you can give yourselves completely to God as a living sacrifice. This is a wonderful expression of worshiping God."

Worship is defined here as a Christian's willingness to give his or her life totally over to God, recognizing that it is His mercy that makes this sacrifice acceptable. Remember, it is a living sacrifice, not a dead one. So these persons, dedicated to God, can make their lives ones of service to God; that is one way they worship Him.

And here's a conjectural picture of an unbeliever becoming convicted of the truth of God . . . *the secrets of his heart are disclosed, and so he will fall on his face and worship God . . .* (1 Corinthians 14:25) Just as the nobles in heaven fall down before the holy throne of the King, this example of Paul's about the reaction of a man believing in God shows the intense emotion of worship. To fall down on one's face before God is a powerful expression of true worship.

If there is any posture of worship that short-circuits hypocrisy, it's falling down before the Lord. I once attended a church service in which everyone got out of their chairs and kneeled on the floor during the times of prayer. I was a very new Christian and was both amazed and—honestly—a little embarrassed at first. But I was also impressed that the church folks seemed sincere in this humble expression of honoring God.

I believe that worship involves a sense of awe and reverence for God, regardless of what position they're in. Different people may express this in different ways, but whatever the expression, it must be heart-felt and not merely lip-service or mechanical ritual.

One final consideration concerning worship: the difference between heart-felt sincerity and contrived emotionalism.

Yes, humans are emotional beings. I think that's why soap operas and some movies are so popular; they've got it all: love, betrayal, sorrow, joy. . . . So how does human emotion fit in with having a great relationship with God, and worshiping Him in spirit and in truth. The following are some verses about the range of human emotions:

- Grief, then joy – *Weeping may last for the night, but a shout of joy comes in the morning.* (Psalm 30:5b)

- Joy and praise –*Shout joyfully to God, all the earth; sing the glory of His name; make His praise glorious. Say to God, 'How awesome are Thy works!* (Psalm 66:1-3) King David was surely an emotional person. Interestingly, he seemed to express his emotions upward, to God, more so than drawing people into his emotional intensity.

- Sorrow, then joy – (Jesus, concerning His death and resurrection) *Truly, truly, I say to you, that you will weep and lament . . . you will be sorrowful, but your sorrow will be turned to joy.* (John 16:20)
- Celebration, joy, sorrow –

    . . As he was now approaching, near the descent of the Mount of Olives, the whole multitude of disciples began to praise God joyfully with a loud voice . . . saying, Blessed is the King who comes in the name of the Lord . . . (Jesus said) . . . I tell you, if these become silent, the stones will cry out! And when He approached, He saw the city and wept over it . . . (Luke 19: 37–41)

And to me, the most poignant picture of genuine emotion is in John, chapter 11. In this passage, which I'll paraphrase, Jesus learns that His dear friend, Lazarus is seriously sick. After hearing of this, Jesus stays two days longer in the place where He and His disciples were staying. Jesus informs the disciples that Lazarus has died. But Jesus then says, . . . *I am glad for your sakes that I was not there, so that you may believe . . .* Jesus appears to have deliberately delayed going to Lazarus, knowing that Lazarus *would* die! Yet when Jesus did go to Bethany , where Lazarus had been four days in the tomb, He wept. (verse 11:35)

This is complex. As a "ministry strategy," waiting for Lazarus' death so that God would be glorified, and His power of resurrection demonstrated to the disciples, is comprehensible, though drastic. And Jesus fully understood that Lazarus would be raised from the dead. Yet when He got there, He wept. It was a deep, genuine expression of sorrow and grief over His friend's death, and suffering, even though Jesus knew what miracle was about to happen.

Emotions are a God-given ability to express our sorrow, grief, mourning, joy, happiness, victory, even anger—in many degrees of intensity. But two words of caution about emotions.

First, unrestrained emotions, even joyful emotions, can get in the way of Christ's work. Mark 1:38 &40–45 is an example of this . . . The passage is preceded by this statement of Jesus, . . . *'Let us go somewhere else to the towns nearby, in order that I may preach there also, for that is what I came out for.'*

Then Jesus encounters a leper.

And a leper came to Him, beseeching Him and falling on his knees before Him, and saying to Him, 'If You are willing, You can make me

> *clean.' And moved with compassion, He stretched out His hand, and touched him, and said to him, 'I am willing; be cleansed.' And immediately the leprosy left him and he was cleansed. And He (Jesus) sternly warned him and immediately sent him away. And He said to him, 'See that you say nothing to anyone . . . but he* (the cleansed leper) *went out and began to proclaim it freely and to spread the news about, to such an extent that Jesus could no longer publicly enter a city, but stayed out in unpopulated areas . . .*

The leper's situation was harsh; his faith in Jesus' power to heal him was real; his joy in being healed was genuine; his proclaiming it far and wide was very understandable. But, it was exactly what Jesus had sternly warned him *not* to do. And the result was that Jesus could no longer go into the populated towns to preach, which is what he said was His purpose. So joyful as the leper was, his lack of restraint in speaking his joy hindered Jesus' ministry in the towns.

Be very careful.

Secondly, I believe there is such a thing as contrived emotion. Perhaps a better way to describe this is emotionalism for the sake of the emotion itself. We express emotion to share our hearts with God and others about life's circumstances—and our victory in Christ—but it can also turn inward so that a person may seek the "feeling" of being emotional, rather than using emotion to communicate our hearts to God.

Worship does indeed involve one's emotions, yet we need to make sure that the emotions do not cause stumbling blocks in the ministry setting, and to guard against emotionalism for the sake of the feelings themselves.

Conclusion: Genuine worship—in spirit and in truth—comes from sincere hearts and focuses on God alone. Worship may be expressed in a church service, a time of corporate prayer, or individually wherever a person may be.

Question 9:

How do I advise people in ministry about the decisions they face?

I LAUGHED AT THIS bumper sticker – "Everything in life happens for a reason. And one of the reasons is you make stupid decisions!"

Well, we want to help people make *good* decisions. As we involve ourselves in other people's lives in ministry, we're going to be asked for our counsel about decisions they're facing. "What do you think God wants me to do in this situation?" "What's His will for me in this?"

It's a real privilege for us to be able to have this influence in other's lives, especially young people, and believe me, it's important for them! It can surely save a lot of heartache, financial woes, and hurt relationships. I'd go so far as to say that being in a position to impart wise, credible advice is one of the great benefits of doing personal ministry because of the long-term effects a good decision can have. It's wise because it's biblical and relevant. It's credible because of the close relationship we have with those we're ministering to. They *will* listen to, value, and consider advice we offer concerning God's will.

As we know, there are different kinds of decisions. Some are easy and quick to respond to, such as being in a fast-food restaurant and hearing, "Sir, do you want fries with the burger?" Even the most devout Christian would probably not say, "Let me pray about that and get back to you."

Some decisions are serious yet require a prompt choice. Seeing a traffic accident and deciding, "Should I get involved in that or not?" means making fast evaluations and a speedy decision. Some of the on-the-spot evaluations might be "Do I know enough first aid to really help, or would I make things worse? Is there anyone else already helping? Is it just a dented bumper or does it look like there could be injuries?" I think God is gracious to guide us quickly in these situations.

For other kinds of decisions, quickness is not an asset. Decisions about where (or whether) to go to college, which job to sign a contract for, whom to marry (!) are ones that need time, prayer, counsel, and seeing what the Word of God has to say. Fortunately, these kinds of choices usually allow us the necessary time to choose well.

Here's a couple of amusing decision-making classics:

College student: "I've asked the Lord to show me if I should pursue a relationship with Kirsten. I told Him that if I saw Kirsten at lest twice a week on campus, that would be God's way of letting me know it's His will."

Me: "Um, aren't you both English majors? Don't you have about nine classes a week together? Seems like you've kind of loaded the deck in your favor ... "

(real story ... so we came up with this saying. "Determine God's will *before* you fall in love, because *after* you fall in love, everything seems like God's will.")

Or this one:

Enthusiastic fisherman : "I see it this way, if I buy the fishing boat, I could have great times of fellowship with the guys in it. I'll even call it the 'Fellow-Ship.' Get it?"

Our key verse for this question is John 7: 17 *If any man is willing to do God's will, he shall know of the teaching, whether it is of God* ... The number one priority for a person seeking to know God's will concerning a decision, is that the person wants to know God's will *so he can do it.*

We'll address this question with an illustration.

In aviation, there is a system called the ILS, or Instrument Landing System. It's used to guide airplanes safely to the runway as they come in for a landing in darkness or clouds. Part of this system consists of four guides: radar vectoring, then three electronic beacons, called the outer marker, middle marker, and the inner marker. Each of these triggers a light in the cockpit if the plane is correctly lined up. Then the pilot knows he's /she's headed toward the runway.

Similarly, to determine God's will, these four things need to line up:

Scripture – What does the Word say, either explicitly or by principle about this issue?

- *Counsel* – What input do godly, knowledgeable people have?
- *Opportunity* – Is there an open door for me to do this?

- *Peace of heart and mind* – Do I have God-given peace that the step I'm about to take—or not take——is the right one? Or do I have a nagging doubt?

First, *Scripture*… what does the Bible say about the decision you're facing?

Sometimes the Bible *specifically* says what God's will is, for example, the issues in the list below. In other cases, we have to determine His will based upon *principles* in Scripture.

"Should I marry Lars? He *might* become a Christian." Answer: It's God's will that you decide *not* to marry Lars, who, though rich and handsome, is not a believer.(or, as the case may be, Matilda, a beautiful and rich non-Christian). Why is this clear? *Do not be bound together with unbelievers . . . what has a believer in common with an unbeliever?* (2 Corinthians 6:14,15)

"Does God want me to talk with my sister about Christ? She is so sarcastic about my faith; I doubt she'd even listen." Answer: Yes.. . . *preach the word, be ready in season and out of season . . .* (2 Timothy 4:2) "In season" implies when it's convenient (or comfortable), and "out of season" seems to imply when it's not convenient or difficult.

Instruction from *principles* of Scripture . . . How about these decisions?:

"Should I change churches? The church I attend is the one I grew up in, and I know and like pretty much everyone here. Plus, it's the church in which my parents have been leaders in for 40 years. They'd be hurt if I went to another church, but I feel like this church doesn't offer good opportunities for me to grow. The Sunday messages are super basic, there are no in-depth Bible studies, and they did away with Sunday school. I really want to be a solid Christian and serve God. What should I do?"

Does Hebrews 5: 12 – 6:1 help us in this decision?

> *For though by this time you ought to be teachers, you have need again for someone to teach you again the elementary principles of the oracles of God, and you have come to need milk and not solid food. For everyone who partakes only of milk is not accustomed to the word of righteousness, for he is a babe. But solid food is for the mature, who because of practice have their senses trained to discern good and evil. Therefore, leaving the elementary teachings about the Christ, let us press on to maturity . . .*

The principle? If a person wants to grow to Christian maturity, then he or she should choose an environment in which growth is promoted. This means "leaving the elementary teachings" if that is what is being presented at one church, and "press on to maturity" in a church setting which focuses on helping people achieve "adulthood" in the faith.

Or this decision? "My friend's a city councilman and has asked me to run for a seat on the school board. He believes I could aid his plans for improving the school system. My friend's not a Christian, but he's a decent man, and I think his heart really is to help the schools. Should I do this? It would take quite a lot of time. Is it worth it?"

This is a more complex decision. There is certainly a case to be made for being a good citizen and concerning one's self with civic duty. On the other hand is the warning in 2 Timothy 2:4, *No soldier in active service entangles himself in the affairs of everyday life, so that he may please the one who enlisted him as a soldier.*

The statement in this verse of Scripture is that if someone is a "soldier" in active service, then his focus should be on his soldiering, not on the "affairs of everyday life." The principle expressed implies a person who is God's soldier, that is, one who is serving God in His army, if you will, he should concentrate on what his Commander has assigned him, not on extraneous matters, even if they're worthy from a civilian perspective.

The person dealing with this decision has to evaluate how he sees himself. Does he perceive himself as God's person, doing Christian ministry? Or does he, in honesty, view himself as a more nominal Christian who's not engaged in wholeheartedly serving the Lord. If the first, Scripture seems to imply it would be good to turn down the request to seek the school board position.

Second, *counsel* . . . The important thing to remember about seeking out counsel is that it is *not* to have someone else make my decision for me; counsel's value is to *inform* me of as many relevant viewpoints on the issue as possible. Counsel affords us many perspectives concerning our decision, some of which we may not have thought of ourselves.

What are the benefits of getting counsel?

- Advice about how to do things better. Jethro counseled Moses to not try to act as judge to the whole nation, but to appoint able men to help with the task. (Exodus 18:13ff)
- Clarifying the pros and cons of taking a certain action. A paraphrase of Gamaliel's wise counsel to the leaders of the religious Council was this: "If these disciples of Jesus are false, they'll die out anyway. But if

they are of God and you harm them, you'll be opposing God!" (Acts 5:34 – 39)

- *Without consultation, plans are frustrated, but with many counselors they succeed.* (Proverbs 15:22)

From whom do I seek counsel?

- Godly people who have knowledge or insight relevant to the issue.
- (Psalm 1: 1) . . . *does not walk in the counsel of the wicked . . .*
     . . . the counsels of the wicked are deceitful . . . (Proverbs 12:5)

Third, *opportunity* . . . Even if the Bible supports a decision, the door for it happening has to be open.

- *. . . often I have planned to come to you (and have been prevented thus far . . .* (Romans 1:13) Was it good for Paul to want to help the church in Rome? Yes. Was it God's will for Paul to visit that church when Paul wanted to? No, because God wouldn't allow it.
- Lars may love Matilda, and they may both be serious Christians, but if Matilda doesn't love Lars, it's not God's will.
- For example, is it Biblical that the Gospel be spread to every part of the world? Yes.. . . *you shall be My witnesses . . . even to the remotest part of the earth.* (Acts 1:8) But is it God's will that you go to Zimbabwe as a missionary? Perhaps, but perhaps not. If the opportunity never realistically presents itself, you can conclude that it is not God's will for *you* to go. "Having an appreciation for a ministry does not necessarily constitute a call."

Fourth, *peace* . . . If the Scripture supports a decision, and the opportunity is there, then we need to ask God to give us a real sense of peace about it. If there is a lack of peace, then we need to question if it is God's will for us.

Biblical example: *Now when I came to Troas for the gospel of Christ and when a door was opened for me in the Lord, I had no rest for my spirit, not finding Titus, my brother; but taking my leave of them, I went on to Macedonia.* (2 Corinthians 2:12,13) Paul, whose passion to share the gospel of Christ was unquestionable, had an "open door" to do so in Troas. But he had "no rest for my spirit," because he didn't find Titus there. So he left Troas and went to Macedonia. Scripture was clear; opportunity was present; but peace of mind was lacking.

How do I advise people in ministry about the decisions they face?

Modern example: Lars is offered a great job with a company in Atlanta. Lars checks it out and finds that there is a very good church nearby, with excellent opportunities to grow as a Christian and also to minister.

It's Biblical for Lars to work... . . . *if someone will not work, neither let him eat.* (2 Thessalonians 3: 10,11) The situation is spiritually healthy and the opportunity is there...But...Lars prays about the job and does not feel peace that it is a right decision. No matter how much Lars seeks God's peace about it, he always feels uneasy about it. Why might this be? Perhaps God has a plan for Lars that requires Lars to be immediately available, which he would not be if he signed a contract with the Atlanta company.

One last consideration about decision making: how do we to decide what to do in the "gray areas" of life, those decisions like, 'Is it okay to drink beer?" "Should I go to movies, or are they a waste of time or a bad influence?" How does the concept of Christian freedom affect our decision making?

> *It is for freedom that Christ has set us free. Stand firm, then, and do not let yourselves be burdened again by a yoke of slavery.* (Galatians 5: 1)

Here is a list of things or activities. Which are okay for Christians and which are not?

- Beer
- Wine
- Cigarettes
- Golf
- Soap operas
- Academic cheating
- *Twizzlers*
- Hooka's
- Video games
- Smokeless tobacco
- Hard liquor
- Music downloads/sharing w/o paying
- PG 13 movies

- Porn
- Romance novels
- The *Harry Potter* books

Some are obviously okay. I've never heard a sermon aimed at demonizing *Twizzlers*. Conversely, I don't think any serious believer would endorse pornography as acceptable. But some of these might fall into a gray area.

Here's a helpful guide for making decisions about things in the "gray areas." I call this the "1 Corinthians 6, 8, 10 Principle"

- I Corinthians 6:12 *All things are lawful for me, but not all things are profitable. All things are lawful for me, but I will not be mastered by anything.* Don't get hooked or addicted to anything. What activities might his apply to? Smoking, drinking, video games, soap operas, others . . . ?

- I Corinthians 8: 9 (All things are lawful, but) ...*take care lest this liberty of yours become a stumbling block to the weak.* Don't cause someone else to be tempted to do something he/she thinks is wrong by seeing you do something.

- I Corinthians 10: 23 *All things are lawful, but not all things are profitable. All things are lawful, but not all things edify.*

"Edify" means "build up," or an activity that is helpful to us spiritually. But not everything we do in life can be constructive spiritually, can it? No, probably not, but we can make decisions about activities as in the list above, based upon this guide. For example, a round of golf every now and then can be good recreation, but if someone gets hooked on golf, it can be bad. The guideline: Don't do things that you know will make you weaker as a person, or as a Christian. Some things may be permitted, but we know they will make us lazy, or unhealthy, or hurt us in some way. Do the things that are helpful.

Probably an overall mind-set on this would be captured in these two verses (my paraphrases):

Don't use your freedom for sinful stuff, but rather use it to serve each other. (Galatians 5:13)

Live as free people, but don't use your freedom as a cover up for evil; live as servants of God. (1 Peter 2:16)...

Conclusion regarding seeking God's will in decision-making could be as follows:

- God's will is knowable, but it may take some Bible study. (Romans 12:2)
- Be willing to *do* His will, no matter what it is. (John 7:17)
- Seek God's peace about a decision BEFORE you do it, not His "rubber stamp" approval after it's done.

A guide for decision making could be these steps:

1. Clarify the issue – what's the decision that has to be made? This seems so obvious, but sometimes the decisions we face are so complex or have so many aspects to them, that it's very beneficial to try to get to the heart of the issue.
2. Do a Bible study on it.
3. Seek counsel.
4. Pray James 1:5 – asking God for wisdom is a great starting point for prayer concerning a decision (Luke 6: 12,13) – Jesus prays all night about which disciples to choose.
5. Ask God for peace of mind.
6. Make the decision! Avoiding a decision *is* a decision. As with the "shot clock" in basketball, paralysis of fearing the outcome (i.e. a missed shot) means turning the ball over anyway when time runs out. Take a shot; make a decision.
7. Set a time period in which you will not change the decision; this helps keep us from getting in the habit of second-guessing, and vetoing our own decisions.

Question 10

What are issues that Christians ask about?

- Issue one: *What's my spiritual gift?*

    First of all, let's define 'spiritual gifts.' The spiritual gifts mentioned in the three passages in Scripture do not include talents or abilities, such as music, athleticism, or a proficiency in math. These are indeed human strengths which God has bestowed upon people, but they are not spiritual gifts. These are referenced by Paul in the three passages in Romans, 1 Corinthians, and Ephesians.

    Scripture states that *to each one is given the manifestation of the Spirit for the common good . . . the Holy Spirit . . . works all these things, distributing to each one individually just as He wills.* (1 Corinthians 12:7&11) Peter's first letter to the scattered Christians adds to this saying, *As each one has received a special gift, employ it in serving one another . . .* (1 Peter 4:10)

    So we see three important facts about the gifts of the Holy Spirit: every Christian is given one. It's the Holy Spirit who decides which gift each individual gets; there's no sign-up list, and no "gift exchange" if a person wants to swap gifts. The gifts are given for the "common good," with each believer using her or his spiritual gift for the benefit of others, not to serve one's own self.

    Here is the list of spiritual gifts, with fast, simple definitions:

WHAT ARE ISSUES THAT CHRISTIANS ASK ABOUT?

From Romans 12: 6–8

1. prophecy – deriving Bible principles, sharing them with God's people
2. service – also called "helping," seeing needs and working to meet them
3. teaching – the gift of clearly communicating biblical knowledge
4. exhortation – both comforting, and challenging to holiness & maturity
5. giving – generously supplying the financial needs of the ministry
6. leading – setting an example and guiding others in achieving goals
7. mercy – showing compassion for those who are hurting

From 1 Corinthians 12: 7–10

1. word of wisdom – communicating a deep understanding of God's truth
2. word of knowledge – communicating biblical information to the church
3. faith – a strong conviction that what God says is true and unfailing
4. healing – a supernatural restoration of health from injury or illness
5. miracles – a supernatural effect for the benefit of others
6. prophecy – deriving Bible principles, sharing with God's people
7. distinguishing of spirits – knowing if something or someone is of God
8. unknown tongues – speaking in words of no known language
9. interpretation of tongues – telling others what a tongues speaker means

From Ephesians 4: 11

1. apostolic gift – going out to minister in places not reached with gospel
2. prophecy – deriving Bible principles, sharing them with God's people
3. evangelism – effectively sharing the gospel of Christ to the unsaved
4. pastors – literally, shepherds . . . caring for and feeding God's flock
5. teachers – clearly communicating biblical knowledge to believers

Let's sort these gifts out into three "functions," if you will.

85

The gifts that transcend the laws of nature, and which are obvious.

- unknown tongues
- interpretation of unknown tongues
- healing
- effecting of miracles

The gifts of the Holy Spirit able to be acquired naturally to some degree are these:

- wisdom
- knowledge
- faith
- distinguishing of spirits
- giving

The gifts which the Holy Spirit gives primarily to be used in ministry are these:

- evangelism
- teaching
- prophecy
- pastoring
- exhortation
- service
- leading
- mercy

The gifts in the first category, the "miracle" gifts, so to speak, are a great blessing when they appear, but in these modern days, they seem to appear rarely.

The second group is certainly important, and are more "normal" among groups of mature believers doing ministry. These gifts, and the ones in the third category, are not only unusual strengths given by the Holy Spirit, but are also *required* of all Christians to some degree. For example, a person may not have the gift of evangelism, but he or she is still told to share their faith. *Do the work of an evangelist.* (2 Timothy 4:5)

But back to our question of how to know what one's spiritual gift is, let's consider the gifts in category #3. We can call these the ministering gifts. When we feel confident we know how God has gifted us for His service, we can put ourselves in ministry situations in which those gifts can be effectively used of God.

Quite simply, I think the three best ways to get a good idea of what your spiritual gift might be are these:

What you have joy in doing . . . It's sometimes the case that God may have you do something in ministry that's out of your comfort zone for the sake of training, but in the long run, He will almost certainly use you in a way that brings you joy. If doing an aspect of ministry does not bring you joy, it's probably not your gift.

What others affirm in you . . . I once attended a Christian conference and met a man whom I immediately sensed had the spiritual gift of evangelism. Every time we went out for a meal, he would engage the servers—even other customers—in conversations that led to what we came to call a "QVG," a quick verbal gospel. This approach may sound rude, but this man could connect with others in a way that was enjoyable and interesting. His friends laughingly said, "Don't plan on a fast lunch. He'll talk to pretty much everyone you meet, so you'll be there an hour, even at McDonalds!" It was obvious to this fellow's friends that he loved sharing the gospel and was really good at it.

What do your friends or other church members agree is a ministry strength in you? This can be a good affirmation of how the Holy Spirit has gifted you.

How God has used you in the past . . . One staff person in a parachurch organization that worked with high school students said that what he really loved to do was mentor younger staff. And as I watched him in his supervisory role with younger staff members, I saw that it was more of a shepherding relationship than administrative. He was very encouraging and instructive, and even protective of them. I felt that his gift was primarily to be a pastor (shepherd) to these in his care, even though the organization he served with emphasized evangelism. And it was in this shepherding role that God had placed him for many years.

As you look back on your own experience in ministry, even if it's for a relatively brief time, what do you see has always happened? What roles and opportunities does it seem like the Lord always has you involved in, to your joy and other's benefit? That could be your gift.

The effective use of gifts assumes a level of spiritual maturity. Just as parents cannot tell, usually, whether a toddler will be better at math than verbal skills, or be a great musician, or a pro athlete, so too a new Christian is an unknown. This becomes much more evident as the years go by.

Conclusion: Find your gift and use it!

- Issue two: *What did Jesus change?*

Why does Jesus say in Matthew 5:17 that He didn't come to do away with the Law? Sure seems like He did. *Do not think that I came to abolish the Law or the Prophets; I did not come to abolish, but to fulfill.* (Matthew 5:17)

"Abolish" means "To do away with wholly, to annul." "Fulfill" means to "to bring to pass, to realize, to complete."

We see then that Jesus was not implying that the Judaic Law was wrong or should be annulled. He states that every single letter of the Law was right and correct.

Paul says, *Why then the Law? It was added because of transgressions . . . Is the law then contrary to the promises of God? May it never be! For if a law had been given which was able to impart life, then righteousness would indeed have been based on law . . .* (Galatians 3:19, 21)

But in fulfilling the Law, Jesus brought to completion *the intent* of the Law: to demonstrate the righteousness of God, the unrighteousness of mankind, and the need for the Messiah. When Jesus comes, the Messiah has come. Thus, Jesus says, after reading in the synagogue the passage in Isaiah about the Messiah, *Today this Scripture has been fulfilled in your hearing.* (Luke 4:21) No one but the Messiah, the Christ, could make such an astonishing pronouncement.

To be sure, much of the Law relating to ethics and morality is relevant to all mankind for all time, but a significant portion of the Judaic Law was ritual, ceremonial, or symbolic. Dietary rules, the forbidding of weaving two kinds of fabric together (symbolic of Israel's separateness), and even the laws of sacrifice for the atonement of sin, were fulfilled by Jesus. He was, and is, the perfect sacrifice, and thus enables people to be free from the restraints of the Law and its consequences.

Paul points out—quite forcefully— in the letter to the Galatians, that the Law was a necessary "tutor" for the children of Israel, but that the tutor was no longer needed in "the fullness of time," that is, when God's plan of redemption is revealed through the birth, life, and atoning death and resurrection of the Savior.

> *Therefore the Law has become our tutor to lead us to Christ, that we may be justified by faith. But now that faith has come, we are no longer under a tutor. For you are all sons of God through faith in Christ Jesus.* (Galatians 3:24–26)

Paul sums it all up in one verse of Scripture: *It was for freedom that Christ set us free; therefore keep standing firm and do not be subject again to a yoke of slavery.* (Galatians 5:1)

What did Christ fulfill, and thus free us from, in regards to the Law?

- ritual sacrifice for our sins –. . . *if we confess our sins, He is faithful and just to forgive us . . .* (1 John 1:9)
- the necessity for circumcision, and obeying Law –. .*Therefore it is my judgment that we do not trouble those (with circumcision) who are turning to God from the Gentiles.* (Acts 15:19).
- "holy" days, even the Sabbath –. . . *let no one act as your judge in regard to food or drink . . . or a Sabbath day . . .* (Colossians 2:16,17)
- dietary laws –. . . *deceitful men who . . . advocate abstaining from foods, which God has created to be gratefully shared in by those who believe and know the truth. For everything created by God is good . . .* (1 Timothy 4:3,4)
- Many more rules and restraints are listed in Leviticus and Deuteronomy.

The release from the Law of Moses meant not only freedom, but adherence to a new kind of righteousness. Jesus "upgraded" the Old Testament commands from behavioral obedience to heart attitude as well. *You have heard that it was said, 'You shall not commit adultery.' But I say to you that everyone who looks on a woman to lust for her has committed adultery with her already in his heart.* (Matthew 5:27,28)

We Christians, no longer enslaved to sin, have been given the power to resist even sinful thoughts . . . *taking every thought captive to obedience to Christ . . .* (2 Corinthians 10:5) This is a radical change brought about by the power of the indwelling Holy Spirit, who is in us because Christ took away the veil from the dwelling place of God in the Temple, and brought Him into our hearts as the new temple.

Perhaps the most powerful evidence that Jesus did indeed fulfill the Law, from the rule of strict obedience to compassion and mercy, is seen in the incident of the woman caught in adultery, and how Jesus responded. According to the Law of Moses, the woman should have been condemned and killed. But Jesus saved her life, and said, *Neither do I condemn you; go on your way, from now on sin no more.* (John 8:11) This one amazing picture of God's forgiveness toward the woman captures the immensity of the fulfillment of Old Testament Law by Jesus.

Why is it important for us today to affirm what Jesus changed? Because the tendency for some—perhaps not us, but some we may minister to—to slip into a kind of legalism, as the church at Galatia did. This is why the Galatians 5:1 statement is critical: there can be a real struggle for some to stay free, to "stand firm, and not be subject to a yoke of slavery again." Some may unknowingly find a kind of traditional comfort in adhering to some rules or restrictions, especially if they grew up in a church, or doctrinal viewpoint, that leans towards being legalistic. These little legalisms may seem trivial or harmless, like Sunday blue laws, but the seed of "out-Bibling the Bible" can take root and grow into more serious issues.

- Issue three: *Jesus said to pray for more laborers for the harvest field.* (Matthew 9:38)

    What are laborers?
    Sub-title of this question is "How *we* can be an answer to this prayer." The prayer being, "Please God, send more laborers."

    A campus ministry couple was transferred to a large Midwest university, and when they arrived, they were presented by the students with a large, hand-made welcome card. The card said on the outside, "You're the answer to our prayers!" But on the inside of the card, it said, "You're not what we prayed for exactly, but apparently you're the answer. . . . "

    Well, *we* can be the answer to the prayers of the saints for more laborers for God's harvest field, by *being* laborers. This is not complicated. Biblically, I see that a laborer for Christ would have three hearts.

- A heart for God – one's security and significance is met through Christ, not the recognition, praise, or material things that the world offers. Here's Paul's philosophy of life: *For to me, to live is Christ, and to die is gain . .* (Philippians 1:21) What can anyone do to stop a person with that perspective? If an enemy were to say to Paul, "Stop preaching Christ, or we'll kill you!" then Paul might respond, "If that's God's will for you to kill me, then it's my benefit." *To be with Christ is very much better . . .* (Philippians 1:23) This total commitment to God frees him up to serve whole-heartedly, without fear or reluctance. *For we do not preach ourselves, but Jesus Christ as Lord, and ourselves as your bondservants for Jesus' sake.* (2 Corinthians 4:5) We too can have a 100% commitment to God. We may not be threatened with death (though some believers are), but we can gladly submit to the Lordship of Jesus Christ for the sake of His kingdom.

- A heart for obedience – not "selective" obedience, but obedience to whatever the Lord asks us to do. Someone once quipped that all good ministry should "Either comfort the afflicted, or afflict the comfortable." Too often, it seems that Christians opt for the comfort. Attendance at church services, the fellowship dinner, the one-day Christian conference, even helping with the church's Christmas tree sale, are "selected," but the early morning prayer time, the evangelistic out-reach, or using vacation days for a missions trip, are considered too costly or uncomfortable. James Hudson Taylor III, great grandson of Hudson Taylor, founder of China Inland Missions, once said, "Our modern Christian emphases are so centered on happiness and warm feelings instead of holiness and hard thinking, that the faith of some Christians is nearer to the Bhuddist's'search for peace in the environment than the tough message of the Cross in history." There is a battle for the hearts, minds, and souls of people that has raged for 20 centuries, but a cautious, evasive Christendom looks for comfort and compromise. It's a strange, wistful yearning to view oneself as a serious Christian, yet have the pleasant things of the world as well. It is well defined by two statements made by James in his letter to believers scattered throughout the Mediterranean world. James 1:22 says, *But prove yourselves doers of the word, not merely hearers who delude themselves.* What is the delusion? James 4:4 doesn't hold back. *. . . do you not know that friendship with the world is hostility toward God? Therefore whoever wishes to be a friend of the world makes himself an enemy of God.* There is just no "safe" middle ground. A person's heart is either to obey God, or play games, and hope God doesn't notice his or her half-heartedness. He does.

- A heart for people – both the lost, and fellow believers.

I once visited a campus ministry office and happened to notice a sign in bold letters taped to the office door. It stated the following:

United Campus Ministry Office rules

1. This office is for business use only.
2. No students may just sit, stand and chat here.
3. When you enter the office, please keep a low voice.
4. Check with the minister or associate present to see if he or she is free – don't assume.
5. We want to help you in any way we can and therefore ask your full cooperation.

On a scale of 1 – 10 as regards making students feel welcome and cared for, I would rate this campus ministry as a 1. I thought the last line was especially ironic, as the sign communicated pretty clearly that the "ministers" (at least those who approved of the office rules) did *not* want to help students. It wasn't at all surprising that when I visited this ministry office, there were no students present.

Compare this aloof attitude to the Lord's.

For the Son of Man did not come to be served, but to serve, and give His life a ransom for many. (Mark 10:45)

And to Paul's perspective:

. . . . have great sorrow and unceasing grief in my heart. For I could wish that I myself were accursed, separated from Christ for the sake of my brethren, my kinsmen . . . (Romans 9:3)

And I will most gladly spend and be expended for the sake of your souls. (2 Corinthians 12:15)

Wow. These comments are breath-taking. Paul says that he has such grief that his kinsmen, the Jews, are not saved, that he'd give up his own salvation if they could be! Can you think of anyone you'd say this of? And Paul's most consistent foes were the Jews. Of course, theologically, Paul knew this "swap" was impossible.

Then he says that he is glad to spend all he has, and spend himself, for the sake of the souls of the Corinthians, another group who gave him trouble. This is a real heart for people.

Being a laborer means having a heart for non-believers (See Question 4 *How to share the gospel relationally.*) Discipleship without a heart for the lost is really just fellowship around the Word. Jesus came to "seek and save that which was lost", and Paul said, "Woe is me if I don't preach the gospel!" (Luke 19:10 & 1 Corinthians 9:16)

Being a laborer also means having a heart for helping other believers. Believe me, anyone who is trying to serve the Lord in real ministry needs the help and encouragement you can give.

Conclusion: Find a way you can labor. It may be leading a small group. It may be an evangelistic outreach at a campus, or inner city, or at the homeless shelter. Partner with your local church and get it going. (See Question 1 *How to get started.*) Then ask God to lead you to another like-hearted person to be with you as you minister. Encourage, challenge and train him or her, just as Paul describes in Colossians 1:28 *And we proclaim Him, admonishing every man and teaching every man with all wisdom, that we may present every man complete (mature) in Christ.*

Then you really will be an answer to prayer.

- *Explain the predestination and free will issue.*

This topic arises primarily with ministry leaders, and the discussions tend to be focused more on the implications of each position than the theology of it. By that I mean Christian leaders want to understand how these two seemingly opposed schools of thought affect people's involvement in evangelism and discipleship.

I'm going to ask the reader to accept a couple of foundational concepts as we get into this topic.

First, that the purpose of the Bible is to be understood and lived out by normal, mainstream-of-life people, not just professors of theology.

All Scripture is inspired by God and profitable for teaching, for reproof, for correction, for training in righteousness; that the man of God may be adequate and equipped for every good work. (2 Timothy 3:16,17)

It's more like "How to Build a Doghouse" than Wittgenstein's *Tractatus Logico Philosophicus,* which probably only ten people understood.

Second, that there are some issues that are not easy to understand, such as the Trinity, the nature of eternity, the question of whether we "change" God's mind through prayer, and—our topic of the moment—predestination versus free will. The idea of the last one is this question: Do people participate in their own—and others'—salvation and spiritual growth, or is it pretty much all God's doing?

This may seem like a question that only seminary professors or theologians would find interesting, but the *implications* of this issue are important for all believers who desire to serve God. And please let me reiterate, this is not even close to a comprehensive treatment of the subject. It's merely intended to be a basic handle for the purpose of interacting with our ministry team members.

Of the multitude of verses in the Bible concerning this topic, let's look at some key statements of Scripture from both perspectives.

Verses on pre-determinism, or God's intervention in human affairs:

- *. . . to do whatever Thy hand and purpose predestined to occur.* (Acts 4:28)

- *. . . there was Rebekah also, when she had conceived twins . . . though the twins were not yet born, and had not done anything good or bad, in order that God's purpose according to His choice might stand . . . it was said to her, 'The older will serve the younger.'* (Romans 9:10–23)

- *He predestined us to adoption as sons through Jesus Christ to Himself, according to the kind intention of His will . . . also we have obtained an inheritance, having been predestined according* to His purpose who works all things after the counsel of His will ... (Ephesians. 1:5 &11)

- *For by grace you have been saved through faith, and that not of yourselves, it is the gift of God, not as a result of works, that no one should boast.* (Ephesians 2:8)

Note: Though the Romans 9 passage does not relate specifically to salvation, but God's preference of Jacob over Esau, it highlights God's sovereign intervention into human life "in order that God's purpose according to His choice might stand."

Verses on free will (or choice-making, volition)

- *... choose you this day whom you will serve ...* (Joshua 24: 15)
- *... as many as received Him, to them He gave the right to become children of God, even to those who believe in His name.* (John 1: 12)
- *if you confess with your mouth Jesus as Lord, and believe in your heart that God raised Him from the dead, you shall be saved ... for the Scripture says, 'Whoever believes in Him will not be disappointed. For there is no distinction between Jew and Greek, for the same Lord is Lord of all, abounding in riches for all who call upon Him ... and how shall they believe in Him of whom they have not heard? And how shall they hear without a preacher?* (Romans 10: 9–17)
- *... after listening to the message of truth, the gospel of your salvation – having also believed, you were sealed in Him with the Holy Spirit ...* (Ephesians 1:13)
- *... For indeed we have had good news preached to us, just as they also, but the word they heard did not profit them, because it was not united by faith in those who heard.* (Hebrews 4:2)
- *... who desires all men to be saved and to come to the knowledge of truth.* (1 Timothy 2: 4)
- *... The Lord is not slow about His promise ... but is patient toward you, not wishing for any to perish, but for all to come to repentance.* (2 Peter 3: 9)

These verses describe people's choice-making about important matters, including salvation. The Romans 10 passage asserts that if people hear the gospel and believe, they are saved. The Hebrew 4 verse states that some of the Jews heard the gospel, but did not profit from it (i.e. get saved) because they chose not to "unite in faith" the gospel to themselves. The 2 Peter 3:9 statement by Peter—of what he believed God's desire for all people was—does not make logical sense if God already knows the predetermined list. Why would Peter say God does not want any to perish if that desire is an irrelevancy?

What does one do with this conundrum? For young Christians, this may well echo Proverbs 18:17 . . . *The first to present his case seems right, till another comes forward and questions him.* (NIV) Simply put, while we know biblically and experientially that persons make choices, we also see that the sovereign God chooses to accomplish His will, and does indeed intervene in people's lives.

Now let's consider some implications of each position by taking each to an extreme.

What's the extreme of freedom of choice, in e.g. evangelism? Whether people got saved or not would depend totally on our skill or persuasiveness in talking people into receiving Christ. If they didn't, we would have to feel the weight of their eternal damnation on our guilty shoulders. Even the most committed Christian might well feel that they are inadequate, unprepared, not smart enough, and psychologically unable to bear the burden of possible failure. "If I told someone about Christ, and didn't do a good job, they might reject salvation. I don't want to be the cause of someone turning away from the Lord. If I don't try, I won't fail!"

Scripture says God "graciously intervenes" in the human story to bring about His purpose . . . *that God's purpose according to His choice might stand* . . . (Romans 9:11) I use the word "graciously" in the literal sense, that is, characterized by grace. It would seem God's grace intervenes in people's lives to call those whom He foreknows will respond to the gospel, leads people to them to tell them the good news, and convicts them of the truth. As one person put it, "God's not going to entrust His plan of salvation to the whim of mankind."

The extreme position of the idea that God pre-determines everything (pertaining to each person's eternity) would seriously erode a person's motivation to do any ministry at all. It's just logical; why would someone risk embarrassment or rejection to share the gospel if it really doesn't matter?

The apostle Paul was certainly an idiot if he suffered beatings, stoning, hunger, shipwreaks, and heart-wrenching concern for the welfare of people . . . if nothing he did had any real effect. And his impassioned cry of "woe is me if I do not preach the gospel" (1 Corinthians 9:16) wouldn't make sense either.

If pre-determinism is absolute—only the pre-destined are saved and those pre-destined for destruction are not—and this is irrevocable, then what do we do with Scriptures such as Mark 13:10, in which Jesus says, . . . *the gospel must be preached first to all the nations.* ? Or Paul's admonition to . . . *preach the word, be ready in season and out* . . . (2 Timothy 4:2) if it didn't matter?

And similarly, why even bother to help others to grow in maturity in their Christian faith if such maturity has no logical purpose? The Apostle Paul said to the Philippian Christians that, for him, . . . *having the desire to depart and be with Christ, for that is very much better; yet to remain on in the flesh is more necessary for your sake. And convinced of this, I know I shall remain and continue with you all for your progress and joy in the faith* . . . (Philippians 1:21–25)

Let's consider Paul's statement. He says departing this life and being with Christ is not only "better," not only "much better," but "very much better"! So for Paul to stick around on earth, there must be an important reason to do so. There is. It's to help the young believers in the Philippian church. But why bother? If it's very much better to be in the presence of Christ, face to face, and everything on earth is pre-determined by God alone, it seems logical that as soon as a person became saved, the best thing for that person would be to go right to heaven.

Our presence on earth, as saved people, is to spread the gospel and disciple others who can as well.

Conclusion:

The exact nature of God's sovereign, gracious interaction with humanity, and mankind's choosing or rejecting of God's love . . . will possibly remain a puzzle for many of us. After all, God told us through Isaiah, "My thoughts and ways are higher than your thoughts and ways." (paraphrase of Isaiah 55:9) Our safest response to this complex issue is, I believe, to simply obey God's commands as we understand them, and leave the puzzles and loose ends to the Lord.

He who has My commands and obeys them, he it is who loves Me; and he who loves Me shall be loved by My Father, and I will love him, and will disclose Myself to him. (John 14:21)

Question 11

How do I find good people to disciple?

IN JOHN'S GOSPEL, JESUS makes this statement, *I glorified Thee on the earth, having accomplished the work which Thou hast given me to do.* (John 17:4)

Since the atoning work of the Cross was *not* yet accomplished, and since the entirety of this passage is Jesus' prayer concerning His chosen disciples—*the men whom Thou gave Me*—it can be surmised that the accomplishment Jesus is talking about is the preparation of the 12 for ministry. The fact that we are saved today is founded upon the selection and training of those twelve faithful ones to continue the work of Jesus Christ. *As Thou didst send me into the world, I also have sent them into the world.* (John 17:18)

It is of crucial importance, therefore, that today we also choose wisely those into whom we believe God wants us to invest our lives, so that the ministry of gospel-sharing and discipleship will continue in our own day.

We can acknowledge, first of all, that just the phrase "whom do I choose,"— in a world of political correctness—has the ring of exclusiveness or elitism. It shouldn't. Selecting the "right" people in this sense is not *excluding* people any more than choosing that special someone to marry is excluding everybody else. Jesus chose the 12 carefully with His goal of getting the gospel spread throughout the world in mind... *you shall be My witnesses ... to the remotest parts of the earth.* (Acts 1:8) It wasn't "favoritism." It was choosing certain ones based upon how God's plan of salvation for mankind would be accomplished. *And He appointed twelve, that they might be with Him, and that He could send them out to preach ...* (Mark 3:14)

This question has two aspects:

First, what's a good, logical plan I can follow to identify potentially faithful folks who would be most likely to come to maturity and serve God?

Second, how do I communicate the "vision" of what discipleship is, not only the costs but the joy and benefits as well? For some, when they hear about serious Christian discipleship, it sounds like a $100 Hershey Bar—good, but too costly.

A simple, but biblical, plan could be these four steps:

1. Lead a small group Bible study and look for the hungry ones. (Please refer to Questions 1-3 ... for more details on getting started and leading a small group).

2. Invite one or two to meet with you individually for one-to-one time with the stated purpose of you helping him or her to grow in faith and learn to minister.

3. At some point, explain the "vision" by use of an illustration.

4. Challenge her or him to do something hard.

Let's see what this might look like.

Lead one of your church's small group Bible studies. (See Question 3). The reason I believe it's better to be the leader of a small group rather than one of the participants, is that it gives you spiritual maturity credibility. Therefore, when you invite someone in the group to meet with you for a mentoring relationship, she or he will be more inclined to accept.

Looking for the hungry ones in the group is, frankly, pretty easy. The bored and indifferent ones are simple to spot. But those who prepare for the Bible study, participate with enthusiasm, show insight into the Bible passage or topic, and generally are teachable ... these are the ones you'll consider inviting to meet with you for discipleship.

Having identified one or two members of the small group who seem most hungry to grow, invite him or her to meet with you, perhaps weekly for lunch or breakfast, to go deeper in the Word and learn some ministry tools. Weekly is probably best, as most American schedules operate on a weekly basis. Once a month is too seldom, and every other week is too random to remember easily. Also, with older church members, I always say the goal is for me to share ministry or leadership skills, rather than for "you to be discipled." It's not a matter of flattery, but most serious church members already think of themselves as being mature (even if truly, they are not).

Thus, the idea of sharpening ministry skills is a more palatable. As long as he or she is teachable once you get going, the terminology won't matter.

Let's assume you've been meeting for several weeks, helping the younger Christian with consistency in the Word and prayer. These times are very relational. Most people really value relationships, and the one-to-one times in a discipling relationship are especially good because both the human friendship, and walk with God, are being strengthened. Now comes the time for a little "vision-casting."

Communicating the vision – I share with the person I'm helping that the goal of our time together is two-fold: to deepen our own personal relationship with God, and also to come to the point where we can minister to others. I like using an analogy to illustrate the concept of the power of an individual's life who is living for God and reproducing spiritually.

Dawson Trotman, the founder of The Navigators, used the analogy of human reproduction to depict the great power of individual discipleship. His idea was that humans having children was how the world got populated, and Christians having "spiritual children" would be how the world would be reached with the gospel of Christ. (*Born to Reproduce* booklet, NavPress, Colorado Springs, Colorado)

The illustration I share focuses on Jesus feeding the multitudes on the hillside. In the account of this event, the feeding of the 5000 (really, as many as 20,000 in total), as recorded in Matthew 14, it struck me what a clear picture it is of discipleship The passage says that, *He took the five loaves and the two fish...blessed the food, and breaking the loaves He gave them to the disciples, and the disciples gave to the multitudes, and they all ate, and were satisfied.* (Matthew 14: 19, 20)

How this miracle actually "functioned" is not detailed, but I doubt very much that after the disciples received the food from Jesus, they somehow made big piles of fish and bread and all the thousands marched past and grabbed some. The fish on the bottom of the pile would have been pretty unappetizing. Nor do I think that the 12 disciples walked from row to row themselves handing out food; that would have taken a long time.

The inference is, I believe, that as each person received some food and turned to hand it to another, the food miraculously regenerated. That way, the 15 to 20 thousand could all have received satisfying food in a short period of time.

Isn't that a good representation of discipleship? To paraphrase 2 Timothy 2: 2,... *the things you received from me, give to others who will be able to give to others as well . . .*

As people are helped to grow in their walks with God, and receive training in how to help still others, the number of disciples grows. In time, many people can be reached with the gospel, in the USA, Africa, and "even to the ends of the earth." What a simple yet powerful plan for ministry.

Here's a true story with fake names. Spencer and Anna at a Christian fund-raiser, met a young woman, Julia, who talked with them about her love for the Lord and her ideas for a ministry she was working on called, "Moms disciple daughters." This young woman was really excited and seemed pretty solid in the Scripture, and how to disciple someone.

Later that evening, a friend came over and said to Anna, "What do you think of your great, great, great, granddaughter?" Anna said, "What!!?"

It turns out that the young woman, Julia, had been personally discipled by Christie,, who had been discipled by Heather, who had been discipled by Carol Ann, who had been discipled by Grace, who had been discipled more than 14 years ago by Anna. Lives do reproduce.

This is just a simple illustration of the fact that if a person lives for Christ, and helps others to live for Christ, they can encounter someone they've never met before who is actually fruit of their ministry! You could walk right past a total stranger in Walmart who's walking with the Lord because of your life.

The challenge – This part of the effort to find "faithful ones" to disciple may seem somewhat unusual. We want to challenge our young Christian to do something difficult. I don't mean something strange or abnormal, like the open air "preachers" on some campuses who scream imprecations at students. I mean an aspect of the obedient Christian life that most Christians would find challenging, like sharing the gospel.

Come up with realistic, modern-day standards and qualities that are conducive to serious discipleship. Let's say, for example, that you ask the person you're meeting with for discipleship to join you and your non-Christian friend for lunch, and that you're going to try to share the gospel with her or him. Or that you've been invited to the Sigma Chi house on campus to meet with some guys, and could your person come along. In either case, you can say, "You don't have to do anything, or say a word. Just come along with me and see how I share with non-believers." If we sometimes wonder how we can motivate young Christians to be passionate about serving God, the answer in large part is simply by doing it ourselves! Your life, lived for Christ, is the greatest leverage in another person's life to move her or him toward serious commitment.

This is, in a way, what Jesus did with His disciples early in His ministry, when He took them up to Jerusalem, went to the Temple, and tore the place apart! (John 2:13–17) The disciples—who might have been a bit in awe of the splendor of the Temple—probably thought, "This is the man we came with! And He's causing a riot in the Temple!" It was enough that they were with Jesus, and identified with Him, as He overturned the tables of the moneychangers. Likewise, it's enough for the younger Christian you're helping to just be with you as you share the gospel: an action most believers find scary.

Later in His ministry, after He had taught some drastic truths, causing some of His disciples to leave, Jesus said to the 12, . . . *You do not want to go away also, do you?* (John 6:67) From the context, it's clear that Jesus is *not* pleading with them to stay, but rather offering them an opportunity to leave. In other words, following Christ is a voluntary choice. If people think it's too difficult, then Jesus basically reminds them that the door is always open.

What's the point? The sad fact is that some Christians are "selectively obedient." They will gladly do the easy things of the faith, like a pot-luck dinner after church in the fellowship hall, but balk at the challenging commands. We challenge young Christians because the fact is, for the most part, if they'll do the hard things of the faith, they'll do it all. If they turn away from the difficult things, or what they perceive as difficult, they are like the rich young man who turned away when Jesus challenged him to sell all he had and give it to the poor (Matthew 19:21,22) Compromise is all together too easy in the Christian life, and we must be wise and discerning so as to not invest ourselves in trying to disciple the unwilling or half-hearted.

I am not implying that we have to be so hard-core that we're unsympathetic. In one college ministry, several of the young men confessed that they were intimidated and embarrassed about talking to non-Christians about Christ. But they really wanted to get over their fear. So five of us jumped in a car, drove to another college about 100 miles away, and literally ran around campus, trying to talk to every person we saw. We called it "Being a Fool for Christ Day!" Our thought was no one knew who we were, and we'd never see them again, so it didn't matter what they thought of us. I have a vivid memory of seeing one of the fellows actually sprinting across a quad to intercept a couple of students. It was quite fun and very liberating!

This day on campus also revealed a lot about each of the fellows who participated. The one person who was the most introverted was the bravest of us all. It was an environment in which he showed that even though he was very shy, he could muster up the courage to do whatever he was convinced God wanted him to do. If we hadn't done the "Fool for Christ" day, I don't think I would have ever known how courageous this guy was. A lot of people whom some would call problem people, or high maintenance folks, are the very ones God would choose, and whom we can choose if we are wise.

I was working on a Bible study one time with a friend of mine, Thomas Gilbert, (*Life To Life Ministry*) and he said he thought God loved to use those he called "the flawed faithful," that is, people who sure had problems and character flaws, but who were faithful to God's plan for them. He referenced Abraham, Isaac, and Jacob; each had issues (especially Jacob) but they were those whom God could choose and use for His Kingdom.

The whole idea of challenging young Christians may seem counter-intuitive, but the idea is not to have low or easy standards in an attempt to attract lots of people. Instead, have high or tough standards to identify serious people. Your goal is to disciple faithful, able ones (2 Timothy 2:2) who will labor, not to get another big crowd of half-hearted ones. I sincerely feel that some aspects of modern-day Christendom is more focused on entertainment than the tough message of *deny self, take up the cross daily, and follow Me.* (Luke 9:23)

And finally, I'll mention the necessity of prayer. Jesus used great wisdom in drawing followers to Himself, and allowing them to demonstrate their faithfulness and commitment. But He also prayed all night before selecting them. (Luke 6:12,13)

Ultimately, God will lead us to those whom He desires for us to meet with for discipleship, and I think that means praying that God would miraculously bring people to us, as well as trusting our ministry strategies to find them ourselves. There have been times in ministry when it seems as though every plan we can think of to find faithful ones just doesn't work. That's when we cry out to God, saying, "Lord, no one seems to want to grow or serve. Please just bring a few who do, and put them on my doorstep!"

Have a good, biblical plan to identify those hungry ones in whom you can invest your life. And also pray that God would bring those people to you, even if it is miraculous and has nothing to do with your plan. We desire to obey and glorify God by making disciples—as Jesus commanded—so I believe God will help us to choose wisely.

Question 12

What's the Bible say about submission to authority? Why does this relate to Christians?

IN THE 1960'S AND 1970's, there were a couple of interesting catch phrases: "Resist Authority!" and "Don't trust anyone over 30." The idea was of course, that no one should tell anyone else what to do, especially if the authority were someone who was no longer youthful. As part of a cultural *freedom* movement, it was very attractive to young people who professed to be rebelling against previously held values and morals.

How does this relate to Christians today? Is there any residual resistance to submit to authority in people's thinking? It probably depends on the individual person and situation, but I think the issue is an important one.

My personal observation of millennial-generation folks is that there is no overt "in-your-face" rebellion against authority, but a kind of polite "No, thanks" attitude toward submitting to another's leadership. The two most notable exceptions to this are submitting to a college professor's authority, and submitting to whatever the structure is of one's job. Both of these kinds of submission are seen, I believe, as mandatory . . . and are seen as beneficial for the person submitting. If someone wants to graduate from college, she or he has to put himself under the authority of the teacher. If one wants to make a living and advance in his or her job, she has to agree to the rules of the job.

But when it comes to one's free time, or discretionary choices, that's when the hesitancy to commit to another's leadership comes into play. As one college senior put it, "I'm glad to learn from God; but I have a problem with being taught by someone else."

God's plan for how Christians grow and mature, however, does directly involve learning from older, more experienced, believers. And this learning means the younger Christian must commit to learning from an older Christian. This is at the heart of discipleship. For example, in John 6: 35–69, Jesus presents some difficult truths about Himself, and (verse 66) "As a result, of this, many of His disciples withdrew, and were not walking with Him anymore . . . " Jesus then asks the twelve disciples if they want to leave as well. Peter answered, saying that no one else had words of eternal life, and that they knew He was the Holy One of God. To follow Jesus was a voluntary decision, but to do so was on Jesus' terms. It meant submission to His leadership and instruction.

It's the same today. If you desire to disciple a younger Christian, he or she must submit to your authority as the disciple-maker, or it just won't work.

Let's look at a few verses of Scriptures that deal with submission to authority.

- *Obey your leaders and submit to them, for they keep watch over your souls, as those who will give an account. Let them do this with joy and not with grief, for this would be unprofitable for you.* (Hebrews 13:17)

    Hebrews 13:17 is perhaps the clearest biblical statement of the necessity, and benefit, of Christians submitting to *spiritual* authority. Though there is some debate on the readership of this book, the title—and the issues considered—indicate that the intended audience is Christians with a Jewish background. Why is this important? Well, in part, the history of the Jewish people is one of frequent rebellion against God's authority. Thus, for the writer of this Bible book to require these believers to obey and submit to their spiritual leaders is very appropriate.

    The key reason for this submission is that those who submit benefit from it. Those in spiritual authority are those who "keep watch over your souls," and are answerable to God for helping the younger Christians to grow. It also instructs these followers to submit in such a way that the leaders find it joyful, not aggravating, to minister to them.

    If you have ever tried to help someone who is fighting you every step of the way, you know exactly what this means. It really is a grief to get with people like this. Their un-teachability and resistance take all the joy out of the relationship. What the person with the resistant attitude doesn't realize is that he or she is getting nothing out of it. It's unprofitable for them, and an exhausting, joyless experience for you.

- *Let every person be in subjection to the governing authorities. For there is no authority except from God, and those which exist are established by God. Therefore he who resists authority has opposed the ordinance of God . . . Wherefore it is necessary to be in subjection, not only because of wrath, but also for conscience's sake.* (Romans 13:1,2 & 5)

  In this passage, Paul emphasizes the *establishment* of governmental authority as coming from God. Therefore, a person who resists obeying governmental authority, Paul says, is resisting God's authority. In plain terms, if a person stated, "I will obey God, but I will not obey the ridiculous 15 mile-per-hour speed limit in my neighborhood!" . . . that person would be in violation of Romans 13:1. This, of course, raises all kinds of interesting questions about, e.g. the American revolution, or civil disobedience, etc. But our concern here is the guideline for Christians focused on serving the Lord, not trying to change government policies.

- *Keep your behavior excellent among the Gentiles, so that in the thing in which they slander you as evildoers, they may on account of your good deeds, as they observe them, glorify God in the day of visitation. Submit yourselves for the Lord's sake, to every human institution, whether to a king as the one in authority, or to governors as sent by him for the punishment of evildoers and the praise of those who do right. For such is the will of God that by doing right you may silence the ignorance of foolish men.* (1 Peter 2:12 –15)

  Here we see Peter's admonition to believers to "submit yourselves . . . to every human institution" as a powerful witness to the unbelieving world. There were instances in which opponents of Christ made accusations that civil laws were being violated. *And they began to accuse Him, saying, 'We found this man misleading our nation and forbidding to pay taxes to Caesar . . .* (Luke 23:2)

  Peter instructs Christians to submit to civil authority so that these kinds of accusations will be silenced.

- *These things speak and exhort and reprove with all authority. Let no one disregard you.* (Titus 2:15)

What a forceful statement this is! Paul tells Titus, who was apparently a pretty forceful man anyway, to challenge, exhort and rebuke the Christians in Crete. The churches in Crete were seemingly in disarray, and Paul told Titus to "set in order what remains, and appoint elders (leaders) in every city . . ." Paul says to do this "with all authority," and that no one should disregard Titus' authority to do so. While this exercise of authority is certainly politically incorrect from a modern viewpoint, Paul knew it was necessary for the benefit of the churches in Crete.

The basic principle, then, of submission to authority—both civil and spiritual—is that it is really submission to the authority "systems" God has put in place. To resist authority is to take ourselves out from under the "umbrella" of God's plan and protection.

This principle can make some people very uneasy. They might well think, "What about corrupt government? What about bad leadership, even in the Christian community? Does God really expect me to submit to other humans who might mistreat me?"

In the Christian context, of course, a person should not blindly submit to just anyone. The Christian who desires to have another older believer disciple her or him, should carefully consider which person to commit to. *Evaluate . . . those who led you, who spoke the word of God to you, and considering the result of their conduct, imitate their faith.* (Hebrews 13:7)

And in the civil context, there are times when Christians should *not* submit to authority.

- When authority forbids what God requires:
- When the early disciples were forbidden to speak the name of Jesus, they did so anyway, saying "We must obey God rather than men." (Acts 4: 18-20 & 5: 28,29)
- When authority requires what God forbids:

In the book of Daniel, the three friends of Daniel are ordered to worship the golden image the king has set up, or be thrown into a furnace. They tell the king that their God can deliver them from death in the furnace (which He does), but even if God doesn't deliver them, they will never worship the golden image.(Daniel 3:12–18)

The "safeguard" for Christians who submit to civil and spiritual authority is God's control over all aspects of our lives. Christ is . . . . *before all things, and in Him all things hold together."* (Colossians 1:17) Jesus Christ is the glue of the universe; there is nothing outside His sovereign control.

Question 13

Can we hurt people in ministry?

THIS IS AN IMPORTANT question, with a somewhat complicated answer. Many pastors, and others in Christian ministry, have encountered people who claim to have had bad experiences with "religious leaders" in the past. The perceived hurts often seem to fall into the categories of "They just wanted my money" or "They judged me about stupid things like my tattoo" or "When my mother was sick, no one from the church visited." Some of these folks would say that's the reason they dislike church or religion in general.

Of course, for some, these perceived hurts are convenient excuses for them not to participate in something they really didn't want to be a part of anyway. But others might sincerely feel they were mistreated—or ignored—by someone representing Christian ministry.

It's obvious to many of us that we certainly make mistakes in ministry that can have a hurtful effect. Years ago, at a Christian conference for pastors and chaplains, the main speaker gave a message titled: "My Five Greatest Mistakes in Ministry" One of the pastors said afterward, "Man, a revival almost broke out when he gave that message! All of us were hugely encouraged because we could relate completely. It's our greatest fear . . . to think we've hurt someone."

Let's take a look at three *kinds* of ministry situations in which people might feel they have been hurt.

First, "ministers" who are in an official position of religious authority, but have no intention of ministering to their congregations. In fact, the hurt done to people by these false ministers is more deliberate than incidental.

- Eli's sons, who were priests . . . *And the two sons of Eli, Hophni and Phinehas were priests to the Lord . . . the sons of Eli were worthless men; they did not know the Lord.* (1 Samuel 1:3 & 2:12) Though they were Levitical priests, these men despised God's law and abused people coming to make offerings to God.

- Ministers who just go through the motions of ministry, or view the priesthood as simply a means to gain wealth . . . *Everyone is greedy for gain, and from the prophet even to the priest everyone deals falsely. And they have healed the brokenness of My people superficially, saying, "Peace, peace," but there is no peace.* (Jeremiah 6: 13,14) "They have healed the brokenness of My people superficially . . . " What an indictment against those priests! The broken ones—whether it is enslavement to sin, woundedness, despair, spiritual desolation—who come to these ministers are brushed off with shallow platitudes. "Hey, don't worry. Everything 's fine."

- Ministers who are false teachers . . . those who are leaders of cults, perversions of orthodox Christianity, or those with a compromised gospel message. *As we have said before, so I say again now, if any man is preaching to you a gospel contrary to that which you received, let him be accursed.* (Galatians 1:9) In modern day times, these cults and false versions of Christendom abound. Obviously, the leaders of cults are not concerned whether those in the group are helped or hurt.

- And finally, the "bad shepherds" of Ezekiel 34 . . . Listen to how God describes these so-called ministers:

> *Thus says the Lord God, "Woe, shepherds of Israel who have been feeding themselves! Should not the shepherds feed the flock? You eat the fat and clothe yourselves with the wool, you slaughter the fat sheep without feeding the flock. Those who are sickly you have not strengthened, the diseased you have not healed, the broken you have not bound up, the scattered you have not brought back, nor have you sought for the lost; but with force and severity you have dominated them."* (Ezekiel 34:2–4)

The analogy is clear. These priests of Israel, who should have ministered to the people, instead exploited them. They did not help or heal; they did not lead or strengthen the flock; they did not go to find those of the congregation who had strayed from God's protection. God says He is against these bad shepherds and will remove them.

And yes, even today there are ministers who eat and fleece their flocks rather than shepherd them. These persons do hurt people, and do so in the guise of ministry, not from ignorance, but purposefully or for their own gain.

Secondly, are those who *do* know the Lord and truth, but whose motive for ministry is either uncaring or reluctant.

Consider Jonah, the original minister with a bad attitude. He really did know God and knew what God wanted him to do. But he didn't like it. He certainly didn't love the people he was sent to minister to; in fact, he didn't want them saved at all.

God tells Jonah to go to Nineveh (capital of Assyria, Israel's enemy – Isaiah 36:1) and rebuke the people so they will repent. Jonah doesn't want to because he fears the city actually *will* repent and be saved. So he flees toward Tarshish, causes a storm, gets swallowed by a fish, repents, cries out to God, gets vomited out by the fish, finally goes to Nineveh, preaches destruction to the city—and sure enough, the people all repent.

It was highly effective ministry: hundreds of thousands of converts from one sermon. But it wasn't what Jonah wanted. *It greatly displeased Jonah, and he became angry.* (Jonah 4:1) Seeing Israel's foes repent and avoid God's wrath was definitely not what Jonah wanted to see in his ministry. But this story is a wonderful lesson about a truth of how God views ministry. He wants to use even people with bad attitudes and wrong motives.

Then there are the people whom Paul mentions in Philippians 1:15-18

> *Some, to be sure, are preaching Christ even from envy and strife, but some also from good will; the latter do it out of love, knowing that I am appointed for the defense of the gospel; the former proclaim Christ out of selfish ambition, rather than from pure motives . . . what then? Only that in every way, whether in pretense or in truth, Christ is proclaimed; and in this I rejoice, yes, and I will rejoice.*

I'm not sure I really understand the undercurrents of this passage. Given the risk involved in preaching Christ in the first century, I'm puzzled why and how some did it from "selfish ambition." But one thing is clear, Paul says he's glad that the gospel is getting proclaimed, whether from pure or selfish motives. So here is another example, like Jonah's, in which people are doing ministry from less than charitable motives, but God still uses it, and Paul approves of it.

And thirdly, and most importantly, let's consider those who know the Lord and sincerely desire to help others to grow in faith. Our concern here is that even though we care about people, and have the truth, we can be fearful that—either from ignorance, mistakes, giving bad advice, etc.—we hurt the very ones we want to help. This is an especially crucial concern because if we don't have an assurance that we *won't* hurt people by trying to minister to them, we may take the path of not trying at all. It's a little like parents worrying that even if they're doing what they believe is right for their children, they'll mess up their kids' lives anyway. That person might feel, "I'm not going to take the chance of ruining any lives, by simply not having children."

The question here is whether to have spiritual kids or not.

Obviously, I'm going to give a resounding "Yes, have spiritual kids!" I strongly believe we can minister to people with the assurance that God will not allow us to damage people as we do so. Yes, we surely will make mistakes in trying to help people grow to Christian maturity. There probably will be hurt feelings, tension, resistance to authority, disagreement, and even some bitterness in the relationships between the helpers and those being helped. But God's plan for how people grow in faith, and His protection of both disciple-makers and disciples, gives us great confidence in helping others on to maturity.

Here are my reasons why I strongly believe this to be true:

The New Testament urges us to do it, therefore, it's God's plan for how people grow in faith.

As far as we know from Scripture, among the last things the resurrected Christ said to Peter was "feed My sheep," and "tend My sheep." The analogy of Peter being a shepherd who tends and feeds sheep, is preceded by Jesus' compassion for the multitudes He saw because . . . *they were distressed and downcast like sheep without a shepherd.* (Matthew 9:36)

We too are asked to be shepherds to those around us. The illustration of people being much like sheep is apt. Sheep have no natural defense, no natural offense, and are prone to get into trouble when not cared for. So God asks those of us who desire to minister to be good shepherds. Here are the things Ezekiel 34 tell us good shepherds do:

- seek the lost sheep . . . i.e. share the gospel
- deliver them from dangerous places
- protect them from those who want to hurt them
- help and heal the hurt and sick sheep

- feed them ... God's Word is the food of life
- make a safe place for them where they can rest in peace

If there is one clear thing I've learned in ministry, it's that people need shepherds. The lost need to be led to the Chief Shepherd, and believers need to be protected, fed, and cared for. God asks us to be those shepherds, knowing that good shepherds do not cause harm to the sheep.

The following passage is a serious charge indeed.

> *I solemnly charge you in the presence of God and of Christ Jesus, who is to judge the living and the dead, and by His appearing and His kingdom: preach the word; be ready in season and out of season; reprove, rebuke, exhort, with great patience and instruction. For the time will come when they will not endure sound doctrine; but wanting to have their ears tickled, they will accumulate for themselves teachers in accordance to their own desires; and will turn away their ears from the truth, and will turn aside to myths. But you, be sober in all things, endure hardship, do the work of an evangelist, fulfill your ministry.* (2 Timothy 4:1-5)

Reread that first verse. Timothy, and we who read the Scripture to apply it, are charged to preach the Word—whether the circumstances are conducive or not— and to even rebuke and exhort believers. Paul tells Timothy the reason this ministry is important: because if he doesn't do this, Paul says these young Christians will fall away to false teaching and "ear-tickling" nonsense.

Another clear assurance that God wants us to do ministry is that He equips us to do it by giving us spiritual gifts. Paul's letter to the Ephesian church says that all Christians are given some type of ministry gift, and some are given special abilities to equip other Christians to participate in "the work of service" for Christ.

> *But to each one of us grace was given according to the measure of Christ's gift ... and He gave some as apostles and some as prophets, and some as evangelists, and some as pastors and teachers, for the equipping of the saints for the work of service, to the building up of the body of Christ; until we all attain to the unity of the faith, and of the knowledge of the Son of God, to a mature man ...* (Ephesians 4:7, 11-14)

As each one has received a special gift, employ it in serving one another ... (I Peter 4:10)

Our best assurance that we won't cause real damage to younger believers is that God's sovereignty oversees the whole thing. Here's the best verse in the Bible, I think, on God's sovereignty. It's what I refer to as the verse Christians *know* is true, but struggle to really believe. *And we know that God causes all things to work together for good to those who love God, to those who are called according to His purpose.* (Romans 8:28)

God is wise, loving and powerful, and has control over life's circumstances, even when it may seem to us humans that things are spiraling down into chaos.

The book of Job illustrates the truth that even Satan must obtain God's permission to bring about the afflictions Job suffers. While we might wonder what the overall purpose of Job's agonies was, one thing is crystal clear: even Satan can't hurt us without God's allowing it, and if God allows it, He is in control of whatever happens. Thus, *all things* work together for our good if we love God and are committed to His purposes.

Given that wonderful fact, we can rest assured that we who love those to whom we minister, and want the best for them, will not harm them, even if we make mistakes in our ministry to them. If they love God, He will make sure that either they will not be hurt or, even if they are, they will benefit from it.

There is a caution:

. . . Let not many of you become teachers, my brethren, knowing that as such we shall incur a stricter judgment (James 3:1)

I don't think this warning, however, is that James is instructing Christians not to be teachers of the Word, but rather reminding them of the seriousness of the responsibility of being accurate teachers of Scripture (as in 2 Timothy 2:15: *. . . approved to God as a workman . . . handling accurately the word of truth.*). Indeed, the writer of Hebrews chides some immature believers for *not* being teachers: *For by this time you ought to be teachers . . .* (Hebrews 5:12)

And there are rewards:

I have no greater joy than this, to hear of my children walking in the truth. (3 John 4)

For who is our hope or joy or crown of exultation? Is it not even you, in the presence of our Lord Jesus at His coming? For you are our glory and joy. (1 Thessalonians 2:19,20)

The joy and triumph of our ministry is seeing those we help walking in the truth, experiencing victory over sin, and serving the Lord.

Conclusion:

I believe with all my heart that God permits us, and wants us, to minister to younger Christians to help them on to maturity in the faith. Through the instruction of Scripture, the guidance of the Holy Spirit, and the different gifts in the body of Christ; God has equipped us to help others grow.

Question 14

Do people really change?

ONE OF THE ASPECTS of compelling stories is when one or more of the main characters change. It's the heart of classics like Dicken's *Christmas Carol*, in which Ebenezer Scrooge is transformed from a heartless miser to cheerful benefactor. Another is de Villeneuve's French fairy tale, *La Belle et la Bete* (Beauty and the Beast) in which both the beauty and the beast experience heart changes. This tale is such a classic that it has lots of spin-offs, even the comedic movie, *Groundhog Day*. Or how about Jane Austen's *Pride and Prejudice*, or George Bernard Shaw's *Pygmalion*? All derive their power from situations in which characters confront themselves and have the courage to change.

But do people, especially Christians, really change all that much? Allow me to throw out two radically different perspectives on this.

First of all, here's the positive reading on this question. During lunch with a pastor friend of mine, I asked, "What's the best, most encouraging thing you see in ministry?"

He summed it up in two words: "Transformed lives!" And he mentioned several examples he had seen in his church family. For this pastor, this was the very heart of Christian ministry . . . people changed by the truth of the Gospel and the power of the Holy Spirit in their lives.

The other perspective came from two mature Christians, both godly in character and strong in disciple-making. One said he was discouraged that he still struggled with a critical attitude toward others.. "I've prayed that God would take that fault away. It's better in that I've learned to control it, but I still become critical so easily. Why wouldn't the Lord change that?"

The other person expressed real sadness that he, as he put it, was "naïve" in discerning principles in the Bible. He was faithful in daily reading, and Bible study, but felt he just couldn't see the underlying principles other people saw. As a young Christian, he had felt discouragement that in his college Bible study, when others seemed to get great insights and applications from the Scriptures, he did not. But he thought that was because he was a new believer, and that this lack of insight would change in time. But he said, "I've asked God for a long time to be able to see the deep things in the Word, but it doesn't seem I've made much progress."

So, what's the answer? Do people change, or stay essentially the same? The best answer is probably "both!"

In some ways, it seems Christians stay pretty much the same as they were before they put their trust in Christ. Hard-charging, passionate Paul who *persecuted* the church, became hard-charging, passionate Paul who *established* churches. His basic temperament and drive remained the same, though his life goal and purpose shifted radically.

In some situations, the change in people is dramatic. 2 Corinthians 5:17 is possibly the best known verse proclaiming this change: *Therefore, if anyone is in Christ, he is a new creation; the old has gone, the new has come.* (NIV)

Some truly wonderful changes take place when a person asks Christ into one's life.

- a relationship with God and Jesus Christ - *And this is eternal life, that they may know Thee, the only true God, and Jesus Christ, whom Thou hast sent.* (John 17:3)
- salvation and forgiveness through his atonement –*. . . . the free gift of God is eternal life in Christ Jesus.* (Romans 6:23)
- mercy in escaping the eternal consequences of sin . . . . *Who will set me free from this body of death? Thanks be to God through Jesus Christ our Lord!* (Romans 7:24,25)
- power to resist sin and live a holy life – *As obedient children, do not be conformed to the former lusts which were yours in your ignorance, but like the holy One who called you, you be holy yourselves also in all your behavior.* (1Peter 1:14,15)
- renewal of our minds to know truth –*. . . you laid aside the old self with its evil practices, and have put on the new self, who is being renewed to a true knowledge . . .* (Colossians 3:9,10)

- good things in this life – *He who did not spare His own son, but delivered Him up for us all, how will He not also with Him freely give us all things?* (Romans 8:32)
- growth and development in Christ-like character, such as servanthood, humility, integrity, purity, whole-heartedness, love, faithfulness, availability.
- even certain aspects of character such as a change from timidity to courage –*For God has not given us a spirit of timidity, but of power and love and discipline.* (2 Timothy 1:7)

Some changes are sudden and some are gradual.

A good instance of a life changed immediately was the Philippian jailer. In Acts 16:28–30, this man cries out "Sirs, what must I do to be saved?" and goes from jailer to Christian convert in a heartbeat. Gospel writer, Mark, is an example of a more gradual transformation. Here was a man who went from fearfulness (the one who . . . . had deserted them in Pamphylia . . .) to fidelity ("Pick up Mark . . . for he is useful to me for service.") (Acts 15:37,38 and 2 Timothy 4:11)

Life changes and transformation are an essential part of God's plan of redemption for mankind. When the Apostle Paul gave his testimony before King Agrippa, he stated that the Lord had said to him, *I am sending you . . . to open their eyes and turn them from darkness to light, and from the power of Satan to God . . .* (Acts 26:18)

To the church at Corinth, Paul wrote of this transformation: *We who . . . reflect the Lord's glory, are being transformed into His likeness with ever increasing glory, which comes from the Lord . . .* (2 Corinthians 3:18)

I think people really change in terms of their values, goals, and perspectives when they become secure enough in their relationship with God to gain humility. Humility does away with the felt need of self-protection, self-promotion, self-deprecation . . . all the "self" absorbed focus that defines so many lives. To be humble is to see ourselves as God sees us: beloved and created as He wishes us to be. It's to have an accurate view of one's self, neither worm nor super-person. This allows people to become teachable, and that's the catalyst for change. Of course, we realize that people need to be *aware* of an area in their lives that needs to change, and then they have to *want* to see it changed. Complacency in the status quo of our character issues is never a good foundation for change.

Perhaps the clearest picture of this security in God is seen in John 13:3. Jesus, *knowing that the Father had given all things into His hands, and that He had come forth from God, and was going back to God . . .* then washed the disciples feet. He knew He had God's power. He knew He had come from God. He knew He was going back to God. We too can have this security: we are from God, are going to go to be with God forever, and that while we are here on earth, we have His power.

But some old things remain. If I had a dental cavity that needed a filling as a non-Christian, I still need to go to the dentist after I have received Jesus as my Savior. And there are obviously other things that remain.

- Our basic personality / temperament will most likely stay the same. Hence, an introverted person will probably not become extroverted—though boldness in ministry can be done by both. In one college ministry, a shy young woman said, "If someone told me a year ago, that I'd be out sharing my faith, I'd definitely not have believed them . . . but it's what I'm committed to doing now. Amazing!" Conversely, a very out-going personality type can learn to listen carefully, treat others gently, or not dominate conversations. Our temperaments may not change, but we can expand our abilities in relationships.

- Another area which seems not to change much is in regard to individual areas of vulnerability. Though people can and should get victory over persistent sin areas, a life-long vigilance is wise for some people with some issues. I don't have a Bible proof-text for this, but years in ministry has led me to realize that different people struggle with different weaknesses. One person may have a tendency to worry about money a great deal, striving to be content. Another, however, might have a lifetime history of never being anxious over finances. Does this mean the first person lacks understanding of Hebrews 13:5, . . . *being content with what you have, for He himself has said, 'I will never desert you . . .* ' Possibly, but probably not. He or she may simply struggle with this issue more than someone else. And the other person may struggle with an issue the money-anxious person has no problem with. Most of us have something to which we are vulnerable, and those things differ.

- And yes, politically incorrect as it may sound . . . an aspect of our lives which seems to stay the same is with regard to how God has created us in terms of intelligence, abilities, creative talents such as music, etc. The Biblical truth is that God has created people with differing abilities, personalities, perspectives as different parts of the body of Christ, for His glory and purpose.. . . . *so we, who are many, are one body in Christ . . . and since we have gifts that differ according to the grace given to us, let us exercise them accordingly . . .* (Romans 12:5,6)

- For the one who felt he didn't have an ability to derive Biblical principles, there are other parts in the body of Christ who can, and they are, if accepted, God's provision for that person who can't. This is how the body of Christ works together for the common good. What I can't do, God has enabled someone else who can.

Conclusion: How does this understanding help us in ministry, with reference to our expectations of people? I used to think that anyone could disciple another in the same way I did. I assumed that if he or she did not, it was disobedience or laziness. My perspective was that Christian growth would cause people's temperaments to change so that everyone could be, and should be, an initiator and outgoing in ministry. I've altered my thinking on that, recognizing some people function best as part of a team with clear leadership to be able to do such things as discipling or evangelism. I also realized I needed to be careful not to equate people's continued battles with vulnerabilities as evidence of disobedience or defeat.

This more Biblical perspective took me far longer to learn than it should have, so I'm glad to share this "lesson learned."

Question 15

What would you say to professors in seminaries?

ADMITTEDLY, THIS IS *NOT* a frequently-asked question about ministry! It comes more under the category of wishful thinking. But, were I given the opportunity, I'd share three things:

The first thing I would say is this: Be very cognizant of the profound influence you have on your seminary students and, by extension, the churches they will serve.

'The hand that rocks the cradle is the hand that rules the world . . . " (William Ross Wallace poem)

If you were to ask a pastor, "What most influenced you in your philosophy of ministry," many would cite a seminary professor, either through life or teaching, who captured his or her vision. I believe that the familiar saying about the hand that rocks the cradle—that is, influences, molds, and directs the young learner—is true for seminaries. The word "seminary" is actually from the Latin word indicating "to seed." So seminary professors are sowing the seeds of what the aspiring church-persons will be. Pastors largely determine what the modern American church is like, and seminary professors largely determine what pastors are like. You teach what you know, but you reproduce what you *are*. So, dear professor, please *be* what you want Christendom in our culture to be.

Secondly, I would say, "Please teach the essentials of the "great commission"

The plan is simple. (Paraphrased)

- *The commission:* As you are going, make disciples of all nations, baptizing them and teaching them to obey all that Christ commands. (Matthew 28: 19,20)
- *The strategy:* Paul says to Timothy, the *things* you received from me (principles of life, ministry and character) *entrust* (imparting something of great value) to *faithful* ones (those committed to follow and serve Christ) who are *able* (have the ability, patience, love of people) to teach others as well. (2 Timothy 2:2)
- *What it actually looks like:* The loving, tender, heart of the mother for her young children: verbalized and demonstrated; and the exhorting, teaching heart of the father imploring his children to walk in a manner worthy of God. All ministry is these two things: love and truth. Truth without love is like surgery without anesthetic: perhaps necessary but too painful to bear. Love without truth is just a sugar-coating of life's issues, lacking the answers. (1 Thessalonians 2: 7 &11)

It's summarized in 1 Thessalonians 2:8 . . . Paul says to the people in Thessalonica, we loved you so much we not only gave you God's gospel, but our own lives as well.

If the pastor does not do this, he will reproduce what he *is*, an endorser of the Great Commission, but not a doer. *Be doers of the word, not merely hearers, who deceive themselves.* (James 1:22) To a significant degree, whether a pastor does or does not do the Great Commission—and teaches and encourages the congregation to do so—is determined by what he or she receives in seminary, and the emphasis thereof.

This is why, I believe, it is so important for seminary professors to teach the "pastors-to-be" to equip the laity for ministry. Ephesians 4: 11,12 states, *And He gave some as apostles, and some as prophets, and some as evangelists, and some as pastors and teachers, for the equipping of the saints for the work of service . . .*

And thirdly, I would say, "Explain spiritual multiplication to your students . . . and demonstrate it with *your* life! " Please explain to seminary students that Jesus' imperative to "make disciples" is given to lay people as well as "ordained" people. The word "ordained" means, at its root, "ordered," and all Christians are ordered to minister, as this Scripture points out: *Now all these things are from God, who reconciled us to Himself through Christ, and gave us the ministry of reconciliation . . . Therefore we are ambassadors for Christ, as though God were entreating through us . . .* (2 Corinthians 5:18 & 20)

Please tell your students that no matter how small or unimpressive a young pastor's local church is, if that pastor is doing the ministry of evangelism and discipleship, his or her effect on the Kingdom of God will be great. It is the concept of the leaven the woman hid in the three measures of meal. In time, it was all leavened. Leaven is yeast, which is a living, reproducing organism. If a pastor, or seminary professor, actually is a Christian who does the work of an evangelist and disciple-maker, and trains others to do so, his or her life is the leaven. In time, many in the church (those who can and will) will be leavened with the inner motivation of obedience and commitment to ministry.

Conclusion: "Dear professor, one of the results of the first Reformation in the 15th – 16th Centuries was to put the Bible into the hands of ordinary people. At last it was believed that lay persons could, by themselves, read and understand the Scriptures that God gave to human-kind. The second "reformation," if you will, would be to put the ministry into the hands of lay people, trusting the Holy Spirit in them to guide and empower them in the work of soul-winning and discipleship.

To a large degree, I think we're still waiting for this second reformation. We're still waiting to break free from the Levitical idea that only the "ordained" priests conduct ministry.

You have much to do with this. Please be a part of this second reformation by teaching, and modeling, the ministry of all believers. Thank you.

Question 16

Why doesn't God help us more in ministry?

JUST ASKING THIS QUESTION seems antagonistic to God, or at best, a lack of faith in God's concern or provision. It's not an accusation against God. We surely don't want to hear what God said to Job about his questioning: *Will you really annul My judgment? Will you condemn Me that you may be justified?* (Job 40:8)

But it is a feeling some of us who have ministered for years wrestle with occasionally. I call these times the "black holes" of discouragement. I find myself thinking, "It's God's ministry! It's on *His* heart more than mine to see people get saved and victorious. So why does ministry have to be so hard? Couldn't the Lord take *some* of the potholes out of this road!"

Here are a few cases in which we may feel discouraged as we work to serve the Lord:

- When we ask for James 1:5 wisdom about people's situations, but don't seem to receive it . . . *if any of you lacks wisdom, let him ask of God . . . and it will be given to him.*

- When we ask for protection from attacks of the enemy of God, crying from the Lord's Prayer, "deliver us from evil" . . . but it still seems as though there's a target on our backs.

- When we ask to see fruit in our ministry—to see people come to Christ, and have God lead us to people who desire to be discipled—but time goes by with little fruit. As one campus minister put it, "We've got a great Bible study, with good Scripture, good questions and interaction—and pizza! Why don't more come to it? Isn't there *anyone* who wants to get serious?"

So, in frustration, we ask, "Why doesn't God help us more?" Here are some possible answers...

1. We *are* ministering in a fallen world, and there are "bad things" that happen to everyone, both Christians and non-believers, both "good" people and bad. It's a normal part of life. *Or do you suppose that the eighteen on whom the tower in Siloam fell and killed them, were worse culprits than all the men who live in Jerusalem?* (Luke 13:4) "Easy' is just not how life is. God knows psychology and sociology, and because the very nature of ministry *is* that it is difficult, a person who desires to be a life-long worker for God, can't be a fair-weather minister. The very difficulty of the work weeds out the half-hearted. *Beloved, do not be surprised at the fiery ordeal among you, which comes upon you for your testing, as though some strange thing were happening to you, but to the degree that you share the sufferings of Christ, keep on rejoicing...* (1 Peter 4:12–13) I have to admit, I still get "surprised at fiery ordeals," but I shouldn't. The danger is that I may feel defeated, inadequate, or—worst of all—that God isn't preventing the ordeal when He could. The solution is to accept the reality, that life and ministry is hard, but God is very much in wise, loving control

2. Serious Christians are "targeted," not only by the enemy, but the secular world in general. *Indeed, all who desire to live godly in Christ, will be persecuted.* (2 Timothy 3:12) And (John 15:19) *If you were of the world, the world would love its own; but because you are not of the world, but I chose you out of the world, therefore the world hates you.*

    Satan's attacks include temptation (Matthew 4), accusation of fellow Christians one to the other (Revelation 12:10)—in order to stir up bitterness and conflict among believers—and deception (Genesis 3:1–5, 2 Corinthians 11:3) in order to derail effective ministry. Our response should not be a complaint to God that we're being attacked, but to be aware that the enemy does attack, and understand *how* he does it.... *in order that no advantage be taken of us by Satan, for we are not ignorant of his schemes.* (2 Corinthians 2:11)

3. There is benefit in times of adversity.

- *Consider it all joy, my brethren, when* (not if) *you encounter various trials, knowing that the testing of your faith produces endurance.* (James 1:2,3)
- *All* (of God's) *discipline for the moment seems not to be joyful, but sorrowful; yet to those who have been trained by it, afterwards it yields the peaceful fruit of righteousness.* (Hebrews 12:11)
- *. . . And He has said to me, 'My grace is sufficient for you, for power is perfected in weakness' . . . Therefore I am well content with weakness, with insults, with distresses, with persecutions, with difficulties, for Christ's sake, for when I am weak, then I am strong.* (2 Corinthians 12:9,10)

We would never knowingly select adversity for ourselves, and even if we would, we wouldn't know what would be really beneficial, as we don't always know where we need to grow. So God's discipline of us as His own children, and life's difficulties, combine to strengthen our faith, endurance, and effectiveness in ministry.

4. God's ways and thoughts are higher than ours. (Isaiah 55:8,9) We may not understand His ways—and it's pretty normal for us to fuss and vent when we don't—but God does not *answer to us*. He does things His way, not ours. So when we cry out for His help, it's really just our frustration being voiced, not an actual request for our will and wisdom to supplant His. Praise God for that! His way is the best way. There is a simple, but wonderful, truth that the pot cannot say to the potter, "What are you doing?" To a non-believer, this may sound restrictive. But to the believer, it is liberating. We understand that He is sovereign: the one with power and authority that is employed with perfect wisdom and love. So we can say, like the psalmist, *Righteousness and justice are the foundation of thy throne.* (Psalm 89:14)

5. And finally, even if God doesn't seem to help, we can put our trust completely in God, for we *know* Him, not just about Him. And that makes all the difference. Even if we don't understand what's going on; even if we're scared; even if we feel that our ministry is more of a failure than a success . . . we can have the assurance that our heavenly Father knows and cares, and is in control. That defines our faith in Him.

Though the fig tree should not blossom, and there be no fruit on the vines, though the yield of the olive should fail, and the fields produce

> *no food, though the flock should be cut off from the fold, and there be no cattle in the stalls, yet, I will exult in the Lord; I will rejoice in the God of my salvation.* (Habakkuk 3:17,18)

Also, as Shadrach, Meshach, and Abednego said to King Nebuchadnezzar, who was about to throw them into a furnace, . . . *our God whom we serve is able to deliver us from the furnace of blazing fire . . . but even if He does not, let it be known to you, O King, that we are not going to serve your gods . . .* (Daniel 3: 17,18)

And in John 6:60ff , when Jesus asked the 12 disciples if they still wanted to stay with Him, Peter replies *'Lord, to whom shall we go? You have words of eternal life. And we have believed and come to know that You are the Holy One of God.'* Did Peter and the others understand the difficulties ahead? Probably not, but Peter realized that Jesus was the only one worth following. He deferred his lack of understanding to his knowledge of who he knew Jesus was. What he knew was Jesus; what he did not know was the unfolding plan of salvation.

This doesn't really answer the question, "Why doesn't God help more?" but it is, by process of elimination, a wise and good response for us to have.

We too can defer our doubts and bewilderment about ministry issues to what we do know: Jesus is Lord, and all is well.

Conclusion:

In a kind of strange way, one of my most compelling reasons for trusting that God's help in my ministry is exactly as it should be, is to look at Paul's ministry. Of all the Christian ministers we know of, Paul is possibly second only to the Lord Himself in terms of effective ministry. He was 100% committed, highly intelligent, wise, adaptable to pretty much any type of ministry situation. Yet, it sure seemed like, from a purely human, cynical perspective, he didn't get much help from God. Look at what he suffered and endured. God actually stated in advance that this would happen to Paul . . . *the Lord said . . . he is a chosen instrument of Mine, to bear My name before the Gentiles and kings and the sons of Israel . . . I will show him how much he must suffer for My name's sake.* (Acts 9:15,16) What a startling, harsh job description. "How much he *must* suffer . . . " Not "might" suffer, but "must."

This journey of hardship is certainly borne out in Paul's own description of what he put up with. He wasn't complaining, just trying to gain a little credibility with the Corinthian church, who were suckers for bogus ministers. This is a long passage, but it's an important view of the nature of Paul's ministry.

> *Are they* (the exploiting ministers) *servants of Christ? (I speak as if insane) I more so; in far more labors, in far more imprisonments, beaten times without number, often in danger of death. Five times I received from the Jews thirty-nine lashes. Three times I was beaten with rods, once I was stoned, three times I was shipwrecked, a night and a day I have spent in the deep. I have been on frequent journeys, in danger from rivers, dangers from robbers, dangers from my countrymen, dangers from the Gentiles, dangers in the city, dangers in the wilderness, dangers on the sea, dangers among false brethren; I have been in labor and in hardship, through many sleepless nights, in hunger and thirst, often without food, in cold and exposure. Apart from such external things, there is the daily pressure upon me of concern for all the churches. Who is weak without my being weak? Who is led into sin without my intense concern?* (2 Corinthians 11:23-30)

I have to confess that in reading this, I think, "If this is how God had it to be for Paul, that man of God, then this *is* how ministry is, and *must be!*" Do I understand why it has to be this way? No. But that's irrelevant. Jesus suffered for our redemption. Paul suffered to spread the word of redemption. And we today will have hardship as we serve also. This reality ought not discourage us.

We can certainly pray—and should—that God will help us as we serve Him. But we cannot accuse Him of not caring.

Question 17

Why don't more Christians do this? Why aren't more believers passionate about personal ministry?

IN A VERY REAL sense, this is the question that can be asked of the Christian world community for the last two millennia. Early in His ministry, Jesus said the workers are few. The harvest of people needing salvation is immense, but those who give themselves to the labor of proclaiming the gospel and making disciples are hard to find. Church and conference attendees are not few. Bible study groups are not few. Even books *about* ministry are not few (!). But the Christians consistently sharing their faith and helping younger believers grow to maturity are few. Why?

The following list of possible reasons is not presented as a theological thesis, but for the purpose of our considering if any of these apply to our own Christian community (including us), and what solutions might be plausible. Here are seven potential stumbling blocks that may thwart the prayer, "Lord, please send more workers into the harvest field!" (Matthew 9:37,38)

1. *Lack of models* – those who actually do "Great Commission" ministry, and serve as models for others. People need leadership to do something challenging. There are not many who are such "pioneers" of faith that they will go out and do such seemingly difficult activities as evangelism on their own. Most of us want a good example, and leader, to take us under their wing and show us how it's done. It's the difference between teaching and training. Teaching is the imparting

of knowledge; training involves learning something from a person by doing it with him or her.

We had a silly saying in college ministry about spiritual mentoring. It was, "Children are hereditary. If your parents didn't have children, it's unlikely you will either."

Look again at 2 Timothy 2:2 *The things you received from me . . . these entrust to faithful men, who will be able to teach others also.*

What if Paul hadn't been a spiritual parent who imparted to Timothy any "things," to entrust to faithful ones who could teach others also, but simply exhorted Timothy to start a process with no content and no strong relationships. Or what if Paul had given Timothy life and ministry "things," but Timothy didn't pass them on to faithful ones? What if Timothy was clueless about how to identify who faithful people were? What if the faithful ones who received the good things of Paul, through Timothy, didn't understand how to teach others as well?

Implicit in this verse of Scripture is the life-to-life relationship between Paul and Timothy such that Paul could give Timothy this challenge, knowing that Timothy would know how to do it. All of these hypotheses illustrate how important model "parents" are in getting believers involved in serious ministry and keeping it going. We think of this process, if you will, in terms of spiritual generations. If a generation has no beginning, no biblical DNA to pass on, no people to whom to pass it . . . then we have an all-too-familiar picture of endless religious activities with little in the way of Great Commission workers.

2. Another hindrance to more workers in the harvest is the concept of the *separation*—not of church and state— but of seminary-graduated *"clergy" and the laity.* (see Question 15)

During a workshop on lay ministry, a church member anxiously asked this question: "Isn't it presumption to think I can 'disciple' someone? Isn't this something only pastors should do?" This may seem like a fairly old-fashioned viewpoint, yet I think many lay people feel the same.

Hopefully pastors will dispel this idea, but that's not always the case. I joined a church elder and pastor for lunch once, and at the beginning of our time, the elder, who had served in this church for years, said to the pastor, "I assume it's okay for us to call you Bob." The pastor looked startled, and replied, "Well, it's probably best if you call me, 'Pastor,' or Dr. Smith."

Why was it important to this pastor that we would not call him by his first name, rather than by his church title? It think it had to do with his uneasiness about crossing the "familiarity" line between clergy and laity, even with an elder of the church whom the pastor had known for many years. This discomfort of this pastor was perhaps pretty extreme, and I know many pastors who would groan at the thought that lay people shouldn't use their given names. Yet there is a kind of residual Levitical-priesthood-thinking, perhaps by both lay people and ordained clergy, that only the clergy "does ministry," with the laity role being to support the clergy financially and fill church positions. This distinction is appropriate for Old Testament Israel. Only the tribe of Levi was allowed to serve in the Tabernacle or Temple. It is not appropriate for New Testament Christians, all of whom are exhorted to preach the gospel and make disciples.

3. *Lack of thankfulness* to God for one's own salvation and renewal can result in not being motivated help others.

There's a story of a little boy who'd received a gift from an uncle whom he disliked. When his mother asked him why he didn't say "Thank you" to his uncle, the boy said, "I'm glad, but I ain't thankful!"

I think there's a big difference between being glad and being thankful. I might be glad of a circumstance or having something that pleases me. But thankfulness implies that there is a *person* to whom I am thankful. There's a good example of this in the Gospel of Luke. It's the account of the ten lepers whom Jesus healed in a village north of Samaria.

> *And as He entered a certain village, ten leprous men who stood at a distance met Him; and they raised their voices, saying, "Jesus, Master, have mercy on us!" And when He saw them, He said to them, "Go and show yourselves to the priests." And it came about that as they were going, they were cleansed.*

> *Now one of them, when he saw that he had been healed, turned back, glorifying God with a loud voice, and he fell on his face at His feet, giving thanks to Him...And Jesus answered and said, "Were there not ten cleansed? But the nine – where are they?"* (Luke 17: 12-17)

I think we can assume with certainty that all ten leprous men were glad that they'd been healed of their horrifying disease. Yet only one was thankful. Only one man turned back to thank the Person who had done this wonderful thing.

Similarly, a Christian can be glad he or she is saved, yet take this blessing for granted. It's a casual attitude about eternal things. The thankful person has an awareness of the incredible value of their salvation and union with God, and is motivated to want others to have it as well.

4. *Unwilling to take a risk* – A hyper-cautious person may think he or she is just being sensible or careful, but in one's Christian life, too much of a "play it safe" mentality is a recipe for inaction.

Look at this passage in 2 Kings 7:1–16, a time of famine and warfare, in which four lepers sat outside the gate of the city and debated what to do. They had three choices, none good, but two were hopeless, so they risked the third:

> ... they said to one another, "Why do we sit here until we die? ... If we enter the city, famine is there, and we shall die also ... let us go over to the camp of the Arameans; if they spare us, we shall live, and if they kill us, we shall but die." (2 Kings 7: 3-4)

When the lepers went to the camp of the enemy, there was no one there, as God had caused the Arameans (Syrians) to believe a great army was coming against them, and they had fled. The lepers looted the camp, then went to tell the king of Israel the good news.

These four leprous men had (1) evaluated the situation; (2) realized the folly of doing nothing; (3) saw the wisdom of taking a risk; (4) were rewarded for the risk they took, and (5) shared the good news with Israel.

Some college students came up with a good application from this Scripture passage. They saw that there were many situations in their daily lives in which they could *take a risk for God*, for example, being willing to speak up in a class (respectfully) in which a professor was ridiculing Christians. They could evaluate what was to be risked—identifying with those whom the professor was ridiculing—and what was to be gained: encouraging other believers in the class. The students saw a benefit for their own spiritual growth in confronting daily situations in which they could risk something for the sake of the gospel, or supporting someone else who was. This may seem like a small action to take, but that first step of faith can sometimes require the greatest courage, especially in the profoundly secular world of the university campus.

It's good to see Christians willing to risk their own image in order to identify with being Christ's woman or man.

5. *Cost of discipleship and disciple-making.* Many choose the easy routes in the Christian community, especially since pretty much *anything* people do is praised and called 'ministry.' While there are many activities that contribute to ministry, anything done half-heartedly is more of a detriment than gift to the work of Christ.

Dawson Trotman, the founder of the Navigators, told the story of one of the first Christian meetings he attended as an adult. A contest was starting with two teams; the team gaining the most points would be treated to a party. One of the ways to earn points was to memorize 10 verses of Scripture, assigned by the group's leader. Dawson, though not yet a Christian, memorized all 10 verses. The following week, however, when the group met again, Dawson was astonished to realize that he was the only person to have done the assignment. One young woman had memorized three verses; the others in the group: none! Dawson's comment was, "It was the first time I learned how a lot of people are about these things." (* Trotman, *Testimony*)

Jesus made clear for His disciples the necessity of counting the cost of following Him.

> *Whoever does not carry his own cross and come after Me cannot be My disciple. For which of you, when he wants to build a tower, does not first sit down and calculate the cost, to see if he has enough to complete it? Otherwise, when he has laid a foundation, and is not able to finish, all who observe it begin to ridicule him, saying 'This man began to build and was not able to finish.' Or what king, when he sets out to meet another king in battle, will not first sit down and take counsel whether he is strong enough with ten thousand men to encounter the one coming against him with twenty thousand?* (Luke 14:27–31)

This passage ought not to discourage Christians from committing to ministry; but it should cause them to reflect on how they will respond when challenges and difficulties arise. Advertisers long ago learned that the magic three words to sell a product were "Quick! Fun! Easy!" Serious Christian ministry is simply not described this way, and those who minister need to be well aware of that.

Talk about paying the cost . . .I was very impressed by a missionary couple who once spoke at our church. They were lay people, teachers, who decided that when their children were out on their own, they'd serve the Lord in whatever way seemed most fruitful for the Kingdom, regardless of the cost to themselves.

The door which God opened for them was to go, first, to rural inland China, then to rural Laos. Somehow, they're able to win the hearts of villagers, learn the language, and share Christ. They've worked and lived for years in arduous conditions to model Christ and share the gospel. The wife told this story…"I traveled to a remote area with Laotian friends. They were worried what they would feed me, but I told them I loved native food. I had a wonderful time, got to share my story (testimony), then returned home." Then she said, *laughing*, "I had food poisoning, of course, for four days, but it was well worth it."

I'm not sure I could laugh that easily about four days of food poisoning. This missionary couple summed up their philosophy of ministry this way:

- Be real.
- Be compassionate.
- Be willing to get out of your comfort zone.

Then they gently challenged us in our culture to also be willing to get out of our comfort zones, take a risk, and tell people about Jesus. Good challenge.

6. *Lack of understanding* of discipleship and disciplemaking. This might appear to be a major hindrance, but really it isn't. Lack of information about how to do ministry is not as much of a problem in Christendom as lack of commitment to do it. I would recommend *Seven Principles of Ministry for the Average Radical Christian* * for comprehensive information about discipleship. For any of us to work hard at something, the goal and means need to be clear. Vagueness in ministry is a motivation killer. (* Cunneen, *Seven Principles of Ministry for the Average Radical Christian*)

7. *Divided interests.* Read the familiar passages of Matthew 6:24 and Matthew 13:22. *No one can serve two masters; for either he will hate the one and love the other, or he will hold to one and despise the other. You cannot serve God and mammon* (money).

And in the parable of the Sower, soil # 3 was . . . *the man who hears the word, but the worry of the world, and the deceitfulness of riches choke the word and it becomes unfruitful.* (Matthew 13:22)

It is such a familiar passage of Scripture, that no one can serve two masters, but I think many Christians try to do just that. They want to be good Christians, but also want the stuff of the world —like soil #3. And, if someone says, "I will serve Him when I retire, or when my family is all set, or…" whatever the conditional excuse is, this person is like the impulsive followers mentioned in Luke 9:59-61. These said they would follow Jesus, but asked "Let me first . . . bury my father . . . say goodbye to those at home." These sound like reasonable requests, but the attitude Jesus picked up on was, "me first," then You. Matthew 6:33 says the correct formula is . . . *seek first His kingdom and His righteousness; and all these things shall be added to you.* The fact of human nature is that we tend to give ourselves fully to that which we have given ourselves to. The kind of "hybrid" Christian who wants the stuff of the world, or to put his own priorities first, is not one who will serve his true Master whole-heartedly. You can certainly serve the Lord part-time, but not half-heartedly!

Conclusion:
Perhaps the core reason more Christians don't pursue personal ministry was termed the "Lordship issue" years ago. It meant that a Christian for whom Jesus Christ was not only Savior, but Lord, sought to know what Christ would have them do, then did it! To these committed believers, Christ was not merely important, but pre-eminent.

Possibly no one but God knows what "ignites" in some people's hearts the commitment and fervor to serve the Lord, no matter what the cost. I think it's different for different people as to what starts that fire going. But one common aspect would probably be the recognition of—and glad submission to—the Lordship of Jesus Christ. Paul reduced his entire goal and purpose of life into nine words: . . . *to live is Christ, and to die is gain.* (Philippians 1:21)

Our prayer can certainly be, "Please Lord, send out laborers into your harvest fields, and let me be one of them."

Question 18

How do I help people in the ministry with problems?

THIS QUESTION, AND SUGGESTED answer, is a general guideline for Christians who are ministering to others, and need to resolve problems that arise in the normal course of events. It's not a deep analysis of the human condition; it's simply a practical approach to dealing with tensions that come up. It also presumes that the person who is ministering is mature and secure, and won't let people's problems discourage them or allow his or her own feelings to be hurt.

In the process of discipleship, all sorts of issues will come to the surface. This is normal and a part of how believers grow, and the one ministering should not take it personally. It's helpful to view every "problem" that arises as an opportunity to minister, not as a disaster or cause for discouragement. Whatever it was that came up was part of that person's baggage / issues, and God has an answer for it—but not if it stayed under the surface. I once told a Bible study group that a motto that I'd adopted was "Troubles? That's wonderful!" meaning I'd learned to see people's problems, and their resolution, as an inevitable and beneficial part of ministry.

This discussion covers a broad spectrum, from helping those with normal everyday issues . . . to helping emotionally wounded people heal (in an environment of safety) . . . to helping people resolve conflicts and bitterness . . . to dealing with those in the ministry group who come to deliberately cause problems, or for their own prurient interests (see "Bad boy" section below).

I'm not going to attempt to offer advice about counseling folks dealing with severe psychological struggles: i.e. bi-polar disorder, OCD

(Obsessive-Compulsive Disorder), severe depression, or any form of schizophrenia such as Delusional Disorder. Our best service to these persons is to refer them to qualified counselors / professionals. This in itself is a arduous task, as it requires a lot of research on our part to find professionals who can be caring, wise in evaluation, qualified to prescribe necessary medications, and offer godly counsel as well.

Neither will we address the reality of every Christian's battle with sin. We all recognize that our fight for victory over . . . *the lust of the flesh, the lust of the eyes, and the boastful pride of life* . . .(1 John 2:16) is a life-long battle for holiness that God gives through the power of the Holy Spirit and Christ's atonement. But that's not our focus for this discussion.

Problem#1: helping those who talk too much, or not at all, in Bible study. Obviously, this is not an earth-shattering problem, but it's certainly a frequent one. It may indeed seem quite trivial, in the grand scheme of things, to worry about a Bible study group member who takes up the majority of the discussion time. And usually, these folks aren't chattering endlessly on purpose. They often appear to be oblivious to how much they talk.

Conversely, there may be some in the group who hardly ever say anything. And when they do get out a few words, they're sometimes interrupted by the talkative ones. When this happens a few times, the quiet ones may clam up for good. This can result in a pretty unpleasant Bible study. Bible study works best when there is good interaction and discussion. When one or two in the group dominate the conversation, many feel frustrated. So how do you, the leader, address this?

First, begin each small group meeting with an ice-breaker question (see Question 3) It can be related to the Bible topic about to be studied, or just a fun question.

Such as "What's the coldest place you've ever been?" Or, "What high school course was your best, and what was your worst?"

Everyone has to answer the question, and this allows the quieter people to speak in the Bible study setting, and it makes the talkative ones listen. Please don't think this little exercise is a waste of time. It's good group dynamics for each person to speak and hear their own voice in the group environment. Plus, my observation is that every age group likes these ice-breakers.

Second, during the Bible study time, if someone is dominating the talk, you as the leader can wait for a pause in the monologue, and politely interrupt. "That's a good point, Theodore. What do you all think about this question?"

You can even solicit other's views by name, for example, "Kathy, how do you see this dispute between Paul and Peter in Galatians 2?"

The key here is for you, the leader, to be willing to intercede for the sake of the group, even if you get a bit of push-back from the talkative person. When you've jumped in and steered the discussion to others a few times, usually the "talker" takes the hint and modifies his or her speeches. This is a good result.

A third thing you can try is to actually do a little teaching on "conversational skills" with the whole group, even if it's really aimed at one or two. I mention that good conversation is like playing tennis: you hit the ball to the other person and he or she hits it back. It's back and forth, with each one adjusting to the other's shot (or comments). There is no barrage of balls aimed at the other person (like a talkative one), or just stepping on the ball and not returning it (the quiet person).

Here's my brief acronym for helping people become more interactive in conversation: it's T. A. L. K.

- *T = think.* For talkative folks, it's helpful to learn how to think *before* talking; that is, don't "process" your ideas out loud. To do so is quite confusing for those who are listening to you. Think about what the issue or situation is, *then* talk.

- *A = ask.* When you've thought about what the issue is, then ask a relevant question that draws out the other person, or people in the group.

- *L = listen.* This seems pretty obvious, but it's sometimes human nature to not pay close attention when the other person is speaking. We can find ourselves thinking instead about what we're going to say next, and miss what the person we're talking to is actually saying.

- *K = keep to the subject.* Don't jump from topic to topic. Don't allow some little "trigger" to get you digressing into unrelated subjects that usually involve you, not the other person. Example: Your friend says, "I'd sure like to find a good, affordable piano." You immediately chase down a rabbit trail with, "My mother had a nice piano once. She loved to play Mozart's *Minute and Trio.* Of course, as she got older, that piece was just too fast for her . . . blah, blah, blah. " Sound familiar? You *should* say, "Ah, what kind of pianos have you been looking at?" This keeps to the topic, and keeps the focus on the conversation at hand, not some vague connection that is all about you. This instruction is especially helpful, I believe, for correlative thinkers, that is, those persons for whom any topic reminds them of other related topics. Sometimes, these folks struggle to even finish a sentence before something they themselves say reminds them of other things. Then they digress, and it's hard for them to find their way back to the original topic.

This little teaching time can also serve to encourage the quiet or reticent ones to talk more, especially during Bible studies. First of all, it helps them to realize that they have good thoughts to contribute. In fact, if they don't speak up and share during the Bible study, they're depriving the rest of the group of some valuable insights.

And fourth, if you have to, you can meet with the talkative one (or super-shy one) individually, and appeal to him or her to give others in the group more of an opportunity to participate.

Problem #2: How do we help people heal from the hurts and wounds from the past that affect them today? These hurts could come from turbulent family situations, frequent moves as a child (e.g. military families), having been bullied in school, illness, and a host of other traumatic experiences.

Younger folks may be affected most in their sense of self-worth, lack of confidence, loneliness, and trouble building good relationships. "Older" folks, especially in their late 30's and 40's (I know, that doesn't sound very old . . .) may struggle more with discouragement relating to how to rear children, disappointment with job situations, sense of failure, and disillusionment with life in general.

Ultimately, it is God who heals the hurt and wounded. *He heals the broken-hearted, and binds up their wounds.* (Psalm 147:3)

But there are steps you as a Christian leader can take to help people heal:

First, make sure your small group Bible study, and other activities of your group, are environments of safety and good fellowship. By safety, I mean a place without cliques, hurtful sarcasm, "inside jokes " or references that tend to exclude people. In short, as unlike middle school lunch time as possible! This relaxed, welcoming atmosphere can also be the tone for the group's fun activities: bowling night, volleyball, or the group picnic. The goal is to provide a place where people can built good friendships without feeling they have to be cool or edgy to be accepted. A group setting in which people can just be themselves, and make friends with others just being themselves is pure gold!

Second, in your Bible study times, have such topics as "Good self esteem," "Relationship building," "Conflict resolution," "Biblical guides for great man-woman relationships." Teaching the Bible's perspective on areas in life that are often troublesome is a very effective "pre-emptive strike." At a later time, when you are discussing a problem with someone one-to-one, you can remind her or him, "Remember that study we did? That verse in (e.g.) Romans 8 was really good."

Third, have personal one-to-one times to share encouragement, to listen carefully (literally, "full of care"), and offer relevant counsel from Scripture. Here's what I usually do before meeting with someone with whom I know is struggling with a problem:

I ask God to help me understand what the essence of the problem is, seeking James 1:5 wisdom about the best way I can help. This may suggest to me a good word of encouragement from the Bible to share to start off our time. For instance, if I realize the person is fearful, I can share Romans 8:15, *For you have not received a spirit of slavery leading to fear again, but you have received a spirit of adoption as sons, by which we cry out, 'Abba, Father!'* Or perhaps a verse from 1 John 4 about love casting out fear. This is not a lengthy sermonette. It's just an encouraging note to begin talking about an issue that is troubling the person.

I think of ways to draw out the person with some gentle questions, like "How's it going with the loneliness you mentioned last time?" Listen carefully, seeking to understand the deeper issues going on. Remember, we're not attempting to be psychologists. We just don't want to give sugar-coated, shallow cliches answers to real problems.

I offer counsel with God's Word, and a strong sense of affirmation.

I call the person the next day, especially if the conversation was intense. Don't give the enemy a foothold to plant a seed of misunderstanding. You can simply say, "Just wanted to see if you had any further thoughts about our talk yesterday . . ."

Problem #3: How can we help resolve conflicts, or bitterness, among people who love God, are serving Him, but have inter-relational problems with others on the ministry team?

Conflict is not always bad. Paul and Barnabas certainly argued about whether to take John Mark with them on the "second missionary journey."

How do I help people in the ministry with problems?

On the first trip, Mark *had deserted them in Pamphylia and had not gone with them to the work* (Acts 15:38). Barnabas, the encourager, still wanted to invite Mark, but Paul definitely did not. *And there arose such a sharp disagreement that they separated from one another, and Barnabas took Mark with him ... but Paul chose Silas ...* (Acts 15:39,40) The consequence of this disagreement was that two ministry teams went out: Barnabas and Mark to Cyprus; and Paul and Silas to Syria and Cilicia.

And Mark apparently became a committed disciple, for even Paul commends him later on (2 Timothy 4:11) Perhaps the continued support by Barnabas, and the stern consequences Paul stresses for unreliability, combined to motivate Mark to serve faithfully (my conjecture ...) At any rate, this conflict did not hurt the ministry.

Neither, I think, did the conflict between Paul and Peter mentioned in Galatians 2: 11–13. *But when Cephas (Peter) came to Antioch, I opposed him to his face because he stood condemned ... the rest of the Jews joined him in hypocrisy ...*

This conflict was deemed necessary by Paul to curb what he saw as Peter's lack of integrity. Peter associated with Gentile believers when there were no Jews around, but did not associate with the Gentiles when Jews came. This conflict also had a good result for the gospel and the Kingdom.

What causes conflict in ministry? Some conflicts arise simply because there actually are bad people in contact with our ministry, such as Alexander, the copper-smith (2 Timothy 4:14), or the worthless men cited by Jude, people who were "shoals in the love feast" (Jude 12–16).

There can be conflict for which we do not know the cause. We are not told what two women were in disagreement about in Philippians 4:2,3. Paul says, *I urge Euodia and I urge Syntyche to live in harmony in the Lord ... help these women who have shared my struggle in the cause of the gospel ...* Though we don't know the nature of their argument, we do know they weren't troublemakers, but co-laborers with Paul in the cause of the gospel. Note that Paul, who was at times very forceful in his dealings with problems, did not seek discipline for these women, but "help."

Other causes of conflict can be attributed to competitiveness of individuals, or between ministry groups—yes, this does happen . . . a lot! Or it may stem from different temperaments, different views on how to do ministry, or resentment at having to do more than one's share.. Martha struggled with this last one ... *Lord, don't You care my sister has left me to do all the serving alone? Tell her to help me ...* (Luke 10: 40)

Resolved conflicts rarely cause ongoing problems, but unresolved *bitterness is* always destructive. One of the enemy's greatest weapons is to plant seeds of bitterness in people due to real or perceived offenses. We may feel bitterness because we blame others for our own disappointments, or because we have come to believe that others do not treat us fairly or kindly. Regardless of the origin, bitterness has predictable consequences.

These are a few statements about bitterness from Scripture:

- *When my heart was embittered, and I was pierced within, then I was senseless and ignorant; I was like a beast before Thee.* (Psalm 73: 21,22)
- *Let all bitterness and wrath and anger and clamor and slander be put away from you . . .* (Ephesians 4:31)
- *See to it that no one comes short of the grace of God; that no root of bitterness springing up causes trouble, and by it many be defiled . . .* (Hebrews 12:15)

We see then that bitterness caused the Psalmist to be senseless—objective thinking and reasoning were nullified—and that bitterness is like a root that grows and branches out, and by it "many are defiled." It is important, therefore, that we seek to help those who are experiencing bitterness toward others, as the acidic nature of this problem has drastic effects on the ministry.

Here are suggestions to help resolve conflicts or bitterness:

- Pray with those in conflict to make sure hearts are right before God, and that bitterness and sin does not have victory.. . . *your heart is not right before God . . . pray the intention of your heart may be forgiven you . . . for I see you are in the gall of bitterness and the bondage of sin.* (Acts 8:21–23)
- Try to get each to see the other's perspective; teach empathy. This is very important. If two people, for example, in your Bible study, are experiencing conflict, you as the group's leader, can get them together and discuss the root of the conflict. Ask one person to explain—without accusation—his or her viewpoint on the issue. Then ask the other person to do the same. Have each agree to not respond to the other's explanation until you, the leader, is convinced that each understand the others perspective. This brings reason into the discussion. If the one reacts too quickly to the first one's explanation, then emotions and hurt feelings tend to take over. If each is willing to see the other

person's position, then forgiveness is possible, even if there is still disagreement.

- Remind each person that the heart of resolving conflict or bitterness is forgiveness.. . . *be kind to one another, tender-hearted, forgiving each other, just as God in Christ also has forgiven you.* (Ephesians 4:32) Psalm 103:8–13 expresses the essence of forgiveness . . . *The Lord is compassionate and gracious, slow to anger and abounding in loving-kindness. . . He has not dealt with us according to our iniquities.*

We need to be realistic, however, about the phrase "forgive and forget." I heard a sermon on this topic once in which the statement was made, "If you still remember the hurt, you haven't really forgiven it." Perhaps this idea comes from the familiar passage in Jeremiah 31:34 (and cited in Hebrews 8:12) *For I will be merciful (God says) to their iniquities, and I will remember their sins no more.*

The sentiment here is, I believe, that God does not hold people's sins against them once He forgives. But it doesn't mean that His omniscience is then limited, and that God literally has lost the memory of the sins committed. I think it's more a matter of *Love . . . does not take into account a wrong suffered.* (1 Corinthians 13:5)

It's not helpful, I think, for us to counsel folks in the ministry that they should somehow have forgotten hurts suffered. They can have genuinely forgiven an offender, and have peace about it, yet still remember what the offense was. The warning signs, if you will, that the forgiveness was not genuine are anger, bitterness, or hatred. If these remain, the one who has been hurt, or believes he has been hurt, has not truly offered forgiveness.

I heard a wise pastor say that the Lord's Prayer is a dangerous prayer, because in it, we ask God to forgive us our transgressions *as we forgive* others who transgress against us. This is a sort of ultimate admonition to people who are struggling to forgive others, but my experience has been that most folks in Bible studies, or ministry teams, actually desire to have resolution and to extend forgiveness. So your role of interceding is usually a joyful one.

Problem #4: And finally, a situation I'll call, "Deal with the guy!"

This is a tough one. It's not about helping a person who *has* a problem, but dealing with a person who *is* a problem.

A young man once started attending our 18-24 singles Sunday school class; we'll call him "Bad-boy." This group did a lot of social activities together, like volleyball, picnics, etc. Soon several of the young women talked to me seriously that Bad-boy was bothering them . . . hugging them from behind, saying off-color comments, asking several of them out on dates to bars, or to his apartment.

I take my guardianship of people in my ministry very seriously. I met with this young man to clarify what our group's rules for conduct were. I wanted to give him the benefit of the doubt, but his response was basically "I could care less about your stupid rules. You're not going to tell me what to do."

He left no doubt in my mind that he was coming to our Sunday school class and social activities not to grow in Christ, but to pick up girls. I told him he was no longer welcome at the Sunday school class or related activities. He told me I couldn't stop him from coming. I told him I could. He saw the look on my face, and we never saw him again.

Does this sound harsh? Many Christians may say they've never heard of such a situation . . . not the first part, where there's a sleazy guy hanging around the Christian group to meet girls; that's common enough . . . but the part about that guy being kicked out of the group. Aren't Christians supposed to be welcoming to *all* people, including guys on the prowl? Shouldn't we pride ourselves on never "rejecting" any person? No! That's exactly the point of the rebuke Paul levels at the church at Corinth. He criticizes the church leaders for not being tough on a sexually immoral man, and not kicking him out of the church.

> *It is actually reported that there is immorality among you . . . and you have become arrogant, and have not mourned instead, in order that the one who had done this might be removed from your midst.*
> (1 Corinthians 5:1,2)

And interestingly, there is some Scriptural evidence that the immoral man, having been expelled from the church, repented and reformed. Paul tells the church leaders in his second letter to the Corinthians, that they should bring a man back into the fellowship (2 Corinthians 2:6,7), if indeed this is the same man. So there may be instances in which this "tough love" has good effect even on the troublemaker.

Did the "Bad-boy" in the situation above repent and change his ways? I don't know. But I do know that biblically, according to 1 Corinthians 5:2, I was correct in the actions I took to protect the brethren.

Conclusion: All ministry is love and truth. Truth without love is, at best, informative, but usually not applied. Love without truth offers only momentary comfort but no real solutions. To help people in your ministry with their problems, view all "problems" as opportunities to minister. Care for people with problems. Share truth from the Word with them. Pray for them. And finally, be patient with them, for the wounds of life take time to heal.

Question 19

What does "success" in ministry look like?

HOW DO WE EVALUATE success in personal ministry? This isn't about vanity or pride; it's about having a means of judging whether we're achieving good results for the Kingdom.

The first sign of success is . . . that you're doing it! No matter what else happens, you are being a laborer in the harvest field for Christ. God delights in His faithful ones and speaks to a person's fruitfulness both in the Old and New Testaments.

> *Since you are precious in My sight, since you are honored and I love you, I will give other men in your place and other peoples in exchange for your life.* (Isaiah 43:4)

> *I am the vine, you are the branches; he who abides in Me, and I in him, he bears much fruit . . . By this is My Father glorified, that you bear much fruit, and so prove to be My disciples.* (John 15:5 & 8)

Of course numbers are always impressive, especially in the U.S. culture, but we're not going to be concerned with that in personal, lay ministry. When personal ministry is considered, small is good. The point is that as we minister to others, we also are seeking to find the faithful *few*, and not worry about the sort-of-interested many.

In a figurative sense, there seem to be at least these three kinds of ministries:

- The "Moses' Model" This is one dynamic leader and a vast number of "children of Israel." While it's true that Moses' father-in-law, Jethro, gave Moses good advice about appointing other judges to help him, it was pretty much Moses and 2 million followers.

- The "Orphanage Model." This is an institution in which youngsters are taken care of, but not parented. There is a dietitian to see to the kids' nutritional needs, a nurse for cases of illness, a director to oversee the running of the facility . . . but no mom and dad. The children basically raise themselves.

- The "Family Model." Here's the kind of ministry we want to have: one in which spiritual "kids" have a loving mom and teaching dad (1 Thessalonians 2:7 &11) This is a parenting ministry, and by definition, it tends to be quite small—and accordingly, quite inconspicuous. It would be very unusual for parents to become famous for having a few children; that's everyday stuff. But it's how the world got populated, parents raising kids who have kids. And because the children have had parents, they intuitively know how to be parents themselves when the time comes.

So as we try to evaluate success in our ministry, keep in mind that we're not so much concerned with quantity, but the quality of our spiritual parenting, which is the best guarantee of healthy future generations.

What is success in evangelism? I believe that success regarding our telling others about Jesus Christ is that every time you get to share the gospel, and the listener seems to understand it, it's success. And it doesn't matter, in a way, what the response is. Jesus used the agricultural illustration of seed planting, watering, cultivating, and reaping to describe evangelistic efforts. So when you have an opportunity to tell someone about salvation through Christ, you may be planting or watering, neither of which has any obvious fruitfulness, but is a crucial part of someone coming to Christ. And while it's often difficult to discern whether the "soil" we're sowing a seed on is hard, shallow, thorny, or good (Matthew 13:19–23) it is success every time you share.

As a side note, remember to make a distinction between *goals* in ministry and prayer *requests*. That is, I may pray to be able to lead two people to Christ this year, but I can't really make that my goal. Whether someone comes to salvation through my sharing is not something I have control of; it's up to God, not my effort or will. However, I can have a goal of sharing the gospel with a certain number of people, say, for example three a month. That's something I do control, and such goals are motivational.

What is success in discipleship? If we can help a few to grow in their faith to the point where he or she has a genuine solid relationship with God, and a desire and commitment to serve the Lord, that's success. Isaiah 58: 10 says, . . . *if you give yourself to the hungry, and satisfy the desire of the afflicted, then your light will rise in darkness* . . . Much of our personal ministry will be helping people with life issues and struggles (See Question 18), and that is very good. But be sure to look for the hungry ones, and give yourselves to them in discipleship. As Paul told the Thessalonians, . . . *we were well pleased to impart to you not only the gospel of God, but indeed our own lives* . . . (1 Thessalonians 2:8)

This life-imparting ministry is what both Jesus and Paul had, and which resulted in the multiplication of believers throughout the world. The concept is simple: the gospel reaches the entire world's population by means of spiritual multiplying.

Here's a somewhat contrived illustration. Say there were 100 Christians on the earth. If none of them shared their faith, or discipled anyone, when the 100 died, God's plan of salvation would die with them. Okay, what if each one of the 100 took his or her entire life to lead someone else to Christ? Then the total number of Christians would remain 100—forever, for the birth rate and spiritual birth rate would be the same.

But . . . what if the 100 Christians walked with God in obedience, led others to salvation, and taught *them* to lead others? Then the physical birth rate would be hugely surpassed by the spiritual birth and growth-to-maturity rate, and millions would have eternal life in Christ. Actually, this is what did happen. At some point in the early Christian church, there were only a few believers, but Acts 1:8 . . . *you shall be My witnesses* . . . *to the remotest parts of the earth* . . . was obeyed, and now there are millions saved.

But there is far to go. The harvest field of those who have not heard is still large, and the laborers are still few. So success is being a laborer for God, and bringing others to be laborers as well.

Conclusion: Our wonderful assurance is this! . . . *knowing that in the Lord, our labor is never in vain.* (1 Corinthians 15:58)

Question 20

How can I keep going?

THANK YOU FOR YOUR heart and commitment to serve the Lord! You are helping build God's eternal Kingdom one life at a time. Our goal is to minister all the days of our lives with joy and excitement.

Here are three bits of encouragement to help us keep going:

Tip#1: *Do little personal Bible studies on your own,* as you come across topics or issues that interest you.

One of the challenging parts of staying strong as a Christian as the years go by is to keep your time in the Word of God fresh.

To be frank, most Bible study *groups* address the Word at a pretty basic level. While these groups may provide good fellowship, they usually don't supply an in-depth knowledge of the more "meaty" Bible topics for a mature Christian. It is certainly true that lowest-common-denominator Bible studies are more inclusive than deeper studies, but the admonition of Hebrews 5:13,14 – 6:1 should also be considered . . . *everyone who partakes only of milk is not accustomed to the word of righteousness, for he is a babe. But solid food is for the mature . . . let us press on to maturity . . .*

I think that the mature Christian can stay excited and growing in Bible knowledge by doing his or her own personal "mini" Bible studies. "Mini" meaning that it's simply a Bible study topic that one can do a relatively quick study on, hitting the key passages and principles, with a clear conclusion. This doesn't mean some irrefutable, definitive thesis. It's not going to be published or preached from. It's just a way for a person to gain Biblical knowledge about an issue or question he or she came across in Bible reading, or as a result of a life issue. The great thing is, we can do these kinds of brief Word studies all our life, keeping our interest in the Word alive and fresh.

Let's use an example:

"Sarah" hears a pastor give a message in which the phrase "we're all broken" is used. Sarah decides to do a quick "mini" study on "brokenness," using a concordance to find a few key verses, and the little cross-referencing notes in the margin of her Bible.

Using a concordance to look up words like "broken," "troubles," "wounded," and "sinfulness," Sarah came up with the following:

- There will always be troubles in life.

    For man is born for trouble, as sparks fly upward. (Job 5:7)
    Each day has troubles of its own. (Matthew 6: 34)

- Honest people recognize their own sinfulness and shortcomings.

    For I know my transgressions, and my sin is ever before me. (Psalm 51:3)
    For I am the least of the apostles, who am not fit to be called an apostle, because I persecuted the church of God. (1 Corinthians 15:9)
    . . . Christ Jesus came into the world to save sinners, among whom I am foremost of all. (1 Timothy 1:15)
    If we say that we have no sin, we are deceiving ourselves, and the truth is not in us. (1 John 1:8)

- People do suffer wounds in life.

    For I am afflicted and needy, and my heart is wounded within me. (Psalm 109:22)

- God sees peoples' brokenness and heals it.

    The sacrifices of God are a broken spirit; a broken and contrite heart, o God, Thou will not despise. (Psalm 51:17)
    He heals the broken-hearted, and binds up their wounds. (Psalm 147:3)
    'I will restore you to health and I will heal your wounds,' declares the Lord (Jeremiah 30:17)

- God not only heals wounds and brokenness, He uses peoples' weakness to His glory and redemptive purpose.

    . . . God has chosen the weak things of the world to shame the things which are strong. (1 Corinthians 1: 27)

God has said to me, 'My grace is sufficient for you, for power is perfected in weakness.' . . . Therefore, I am well content with weakness, with insults, with distress, with persecutions, with difficulties, for Christ's sake, for when I am weak, then I am strong. (2 Corinthians 12:9,10)

So "Sarah's" conclusion to this little study in the Word is this: that people are indeed broken in the sense that life has lots of troubles, that sinfulness brings it's own grief, and that many are emotionally wounded. But God not only heals brokenness and gives victory, but actually uses the weakness of men and women for His glory.

Total time for "Sarah" to do this mini-study was about 1 ½ hours. And what an encouragement it was.

Tip #2: *Have two or three like-minded others* to labor with, especially in evangelism.

> *Two are better than one because they have a good return for their labor. For if either of them falls, the one will lift up his companion. But woe to the one who falls when there is not another to lift him up.* (Ecclesiastes. 4:9,10)

It's challenging enough to stay faithful in sharing the gospel and trying to help younger believers grow, without trying to do it alone. Jesus sent the early disciples out in pairs, and even Paul, committed and dedicated as he was, didn't minister by himself. We have seen over the years that there is a real sense of loneliness—even isolation—for those engaged in serious ministry without others joining in.

How do we find these co-laborers? It may take some effort. As Jesus said, ... the laborers are few" . . . but they do exist! One good plan is to get the word out at your church or small group that you are serious about doing some ministry, and would be glad to have a friend to join you in that. Explain that this ministry will focus on two things: sharing the gospel and helping interested young Christians to grow.

That first part, sharing the gospel, will keep pretty much all the half-hearted ones from volunteering. Jesus knew that there will be those who are curious but not committed.. . . . *many believed in His name, beholding His signs which He was doing. But Jesus, on His part, was not entrusting Himself to them, for He knew all men.* (John 2:23–24)

If one or two say they'd like to hear more about what you have in mind, actually *do* with them what you want your ministry to be, rather than talk to them about it. For example, take someone out to talk to people at some nearby apartments (See Question 4 for more on this). Tell him or her that they don't have to do or say anything; you'll do all the talking. All they have to do is just be with you. It's both scary and exciting. God will go with you, and your friend will see the power of the Word of God as you share.

If you never see that person again, then Amen! . . . you know it wouldn't have worked anyway. People basically select themselves in or out of ministry. But if she or he responded well, and said "Let's do this again!" – you probably have a good co-laborer.

Have, in essence, a little team of two or three who are with you in this exciting work. It's not elitism. It's the solid camaraderie of those willing to do a challenging but joyful work for the Lord.

And Tip #3 is this: – *Don't change!* That is, don't keep shifting focus or goals, trying to find a "better way" to minister. Do what is biblical and what you know God wants you to do . . . and trust the results to Him. It's great to fine-tune ministry approaches, or adjust a bit to a changing culture, but stick with your essential principles of ministry.

For example, in my ministry, I and others have for many years gone out to student apartments at a nearby university, to talk with students and get their opinions on spiritual matters. The vast majority of collegians love to voice their thoughts about how they perceive religion. We have a brief set of questions to get the conversation going, and try to draw students out rather than telling them what *we* think. It is not offensive, and many students have said something to the effect of "This has been good; glad you guys came."

At the end of the time, we ask if he or she would like to see a fast illustration that gives the essential idea of what the Christian faith is. Many say "sure."

It's very interesting and fun to do this. However, we seldom see any immediate results in terms of students making a decision to accept Christ. Why? We estimated at one time that 70% of the young people we share with are non-churched, and most are not even familiar with John 3:16 when we share the gospel. So this evangelism activity is primarily seed-planting, not reaping. One pastor who went with me said "Don't you get discouraged from not seeing anything happen?" From that perspective, it might seem smart to do something else.

Yet we are *not* discouraged. We know that almost all of the people we get to share the Gospel with would probably never go to a church where they'd hear the gospel message. So every time we get to share, we rejoice that the imperishable seed of the Word has been sown in another life. So we're not going to change this activity. Paul said, . . . *do the work of an evangelist* . . . (2 Timothy 4:5)

The same is true for our commitment to one-on-one discipling. Jesus said, . . . *make disciples* . . . (Matthew 28:19)

These two imperatives are clear, and our commitment to them is the way we are assured that this ministry is pleasing to God. We'll keep doing it and leave the eternal results to God.

Find your vehicle for ministry. Make sure it's biblical, effective, and connects with people—then keep at it!

Key idea . . . *Be steadfast, immovable, always abounding in the work of the Lord, knowing that in the Lord, your labor is never in vain.* (1 Corinthians 15:58)

I say again . . . *in the Lord, your labor is never in vain.*

Please labor.

Conclusion:

I trust these 20 brief considerations of ministry issues will encourage you in your service to the Lord. Thank you for your love of God and your dedication to serve Him all the days of your life!

Please feel free to contact the author with any questions you may have about Christian ministry, at www.LTLcunneen@gmail.com

Bibliography

Cunneen, James, *Seven Principle of Ministry for the Average Radical Christian*, Wipf and Stock, Eugene, Oregon, 2011

Guggenheim, Davis, and Gore, Al, *An Inconvenient Truth*, 2006 Documentary based upon Al Gore's lecture series on the topic of global warming.

Hawking, Stephen, Interview with Pablo Jaurequi, *El Mundo*, September 23, 2014

Also, C/Net News, September 26, 2014, Matyszczyk, Chris, "Stephen Hawking Makes It Clear: There Is No God."

Katz, Emily Tass, "Writer Slams 'Fact-Checking' Films as Misunderstanding of Art," Huffington Post, January 8, 2015

Life On Earth, Sinauer Associates, Inc., 1975, Chapter 28, p. 769

Ryrie, Charles, The Ryrie Study Bible, Moody, Chicago, Illinois, p. vii

Skinner, Betty Lee, *Daws*, 1974, Zondervan, Grand Rapids, Michigan, p. 270

Trotman, Dawson, "Testimony," Navpress, Colorado Springs, Colorado